A Markov Chain Analysis of the Movements of Juvenile Salmonids in the Forebay of McNary Dam, Washington and Oregon, 2006–09

By Noah S. Adams and Tyson W. Hatton

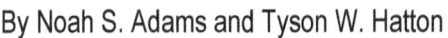

Prepared in cooperation with the U.S. Army Corps of Engineers

Open-File Report 2012-1119

U.S. Department of the Interior
U.S. Geological Survey

U.S. Department of the Interior
KEN SALAZAR, Secretary

U.S. Geological Survey
Marcia K. McNutt, Director

U.S. Geological Survey, Reston, Virginia: 2012

For more information on the USGS—the Federal source for science about the Earth,
its natural and living resources, natural hazards, and the environment,
visit http://www.usgs.gov or call 1–888–ASK–USGS.

For an overview of USGS information products, including maps, imagery, and publications,
visit http://www.usgs.gov/pubprod

To order this and other USGS information products, visit http://store.usgs.gov

Suggested citation:
Adams, N.S., and Hatton, T.W., 2012, A Markov chain analysis of the movements of juvenile salmonids in the forebay of McNary Dam, Washington and Oregon, 2006–09: U.S. Geological Survey Open-File Report 2012–1119, 102 p.

Contents

Figures

Tables

Conversion Factors, Datums, Abbreviations, and Acronyms

Conversion Factors

Inch/Pound to SI

Multiply	By	To obtain
	Flow rate	
cubic foot per second (ft^3/s)	0.02832	cubic meter per second (m^3/s)

SI to Inch/Pound

Multiply	By	To obtain
	Length	
millimeter (mm)	0.03937	inch (in.)
meter (m)	3.281	foot (ft)
kilometer (km)	0.6214	mile (mi)
	Mass	
gram (g)	0.03527	ounce, avoirdupois (oz.)

Temperature in degrees Celsius (°C) may be converted to degrees Fahrenheit (°F) as follows:
$$°F=(1.8\times°C)+32.$$

Datums

Horizontal coordinate information is referenced to the World Geodetic System of 1984 (WGS84).
Vertical coordinate information is referenced to the National Geodetic Vertical Datum of 1929 (NGVD 29).

Abbreviations and Acronyms

ATDL	acoustic tag data loggers
ATR	acoustic tag receiver
kcfs	1,000 ft^3/s
PIT	passive integrated transponder
rkm	river kilometer
SI	modern metric system
TSW	temporary spillway weir
USGS	U.S. Geological Survey

A Markov Chain Analysis of the Movement of Juvenile Salmonids in the Forebay of McNary Dam, 2006–09

By Noah S. Adams and Tyson W. Hatton

Abstract

Passage and survival data for yearling and subyearling Chinook salmon and juvenile steelhead were collected at McNary Dam between 2006 and 2009. These data have provided critical information for resource managers to implement structural and operational changes designed to improve the survival of juvenile salmonids as they migrate past the dam. Much of the information collected at McNary Dam was in the form of three-dimensional tracks of fish movements in the forebay. These data depicted the behavior of multiple species (in three dimensions) during different diel periods, spill conditions, powerhouse operations, and test configurations of the surface bypass structures (temporary spillway weirs; TSWs). One of the challenges in reporting three-dimensional results is presenting the information in a manner that allows interested parties to summarize the behavior of many fish over many different conditions across multiple years. To accomplish this, we investigated the feasibility of using a Markov chain analysis to characterize fish movement patterns in the forebay of McNary Dam. The Markov chain analysis is one way that can be used to summarize numerically the behavior of fish in the forebay.

Numerically summarizing the behavior of juvenile salmonids in the forebay of McNary Dam using the Markov chain analysis allowed us to confirm what had been previously summarized using visualization software. For example, proportions of yearling and subyearling Chinook salmon passing the three powerhouse areas was often greater in the southern and middle areas, compared to the northern area. The opposite generally was observed for steelhead. Results of this analysis also allowed us to confirm and quantify the extent of milling behavior that had been observed for steelhead. For fish that were first detected in the powerhouse region, less than 0.10 of the steelhead, on average, passed within each of the powerhouse areas. Instead, steelhead transitioned to adjoining areas in the spillway before passing the dam. In comparison, greater than 0.20 of the Chinook salmon passed within the powerhouse areas. Less milling behavior was observed for all species for fish that first approached the spillway. Compared to the powerhouse areas, a higher proportion of fish, regardless of species, passed the spillway areas and fewer transitioned to adjoining areas in the powerhouse.

In addition to quantifying what had been previously speculated about the behavior of fish in the forebay of McNary Dam, the Markov chain analysis refined our understanding of how fish behavior and passage can be influenced by changes to the operations and structure of McNary Dam. For example, the addition of TSWs to the spillway area clearly influenced the passage of fish. Previous results have been reported showing that TSWs increased the number of fish passing through non-turbine routes and the fish-track videos indicated, in general, how fish behaved before passing through the TSWs. However, the analysis presented in this report allowed us to better understand how fish moved across the face of the dam before passing the TSWs and provided a way to quantify the effect of TSW location. Installation of the TSWs in bays 22 and 20 clearly increased passage proportions through the southern one-third of the spillway area for all species, most significantly for steelhead. When the TSWs were moved to bays 19 and 20 in 2008, overall passage through the southern one-third of the spillway remained higher than 2006, but decreased from what was observed in 2007. Shifting the TSWs to the north decreased the proportion of fish passing through the TSWs and increased the number of fish that moved to adjoining areas before passing the dam.

Perhaps the most interesting new information to come out of the two-step Markov chain analysis relates to how the performance of the TSWs was influenced by their proximity to the powerhouse. During 2007, the highest proportion of fish passing through TSW22 was for fish that transitioned from the powerhouse area. In contrast, a relatively low proportion of fish passed through TSW20 after coming from the powerhouse area. Instead, the proportion of fish that passed TSW20 after coming from the northern part of the spillway was twice as high as the proportion of fish that passed through TSW20 after coming from the powerhouse. During 2008, the TSW in bay 22 was moved to bay 19, leaving the TSW in bay 20 as the one closest to the powerhouse. As was the case when a TSW was located in bay 22; the proportion of fish passing TSW20 after coming from the powerhouse was greater than the proportion of fish passing through TSW20 after coming from the northern part of the spillway. Passage proportions for fish passing through TSW19, the farthest north of the two TSWs during 2008, was higher for fish that came from the northern part of the spillway compared to the proportion of fish that passed through TSW19 after coming from the powerhouse.

The Markov chain analysis provided a mathematical way to characterize fish behavior in the forebay of McNary Dam and helped refine our understanding of how fish movements were influenced by operational and structural changes at McNary Dam. The Markov chain analysis also could be used to examine how future structural and operational changes proposed for McNary Dam might influence the passage of juvenile salmonids.

Introduction

As juvenile salmon (*Oncorhynchus spp.*) and steelhead (*O. mykiss*) migrate from their natal streams to the ocean, they are subject to both natural and human-caused mortality. Avian and piscivorous predators contribute to total natural mortality, but hydroelectric projects on the Snake and Columbia Rivers also are sources of mortality for migrating juvenile fish. Studies conducted at McNary Dam between 2002 and 2005 provided baseline passage and survival information under typical dam operations (Axel and others, 2004a, 2004b; Perry and others, 2006, 2007a). These studies found that non-turbine passage routes, such as the spillway and juvenile bypass system, provided higher survival compared to the turbines. Additional studies at Lower Granite Dam showed that surface passage structures appear to be a safe alternative to passage through the turbines (Plumb and others, 2004; Beeman and others, 2007; Perry and others, 2007b; Puls and others, 2008). As a result of these studies, surface bypass structures (temporary spillway weirs; TSWs) were installed at McNary Dam and performance tests were conducted in 2007, 2008, and 2009.

The 8 years of study at McNary Dam (2002–09) provided information that aided in developing management strategies to maximize passage and survival of juvenile salmonids passing the dam while meeting regional hydroelectric power generation needs. Research from the annual studies conducted at McNary Dam between 2006 and 2009 have been synthesized and presented in a single report (Adams and Evans, 2011). Summarizing the annual information in a single document is expected to provide a useful reference for managers during the development of long-term management strategies for McNary Dam.

Although these annual studies provided valuable information, important questions remain unanswered. Managers are often interested in understanding how rates of survival and passage vary with environmental conditions, such as total river discharge or distribution of discharge across possible passage routes. Understanding how survival or passage varies in response to dam operations requires data for a wide range of conditions. Studies conducted in a single year only considers a narrow range of environmental conditions, because of natural year-to-year variation in the environment. Multiyear analyses are better suited to developing quantitative relationships than are single-year analyses, because operational and environmental variation typically will be higher over a period of 5–10 years than within any given year. Furthermore, multiyear analyses benefit from the large sample sizes over multiple years, which can reduce statistical uncertainty and help to identify relations that might otherwise be statistically undetectable. We analyzed 6 years (2004–09) of passage and survival data collected at McNary Dam to determine how dam operations and environmental conditions affect passage and survival of juvenile salmonids. The results of that analysis are presented in a separate report (Adams and others, 2011).

Much of what was learned from the information collected at McNary Dam was acquired from analyses of three-dimensional (hereafter referred to as 3-D) tracks of fish movements in the forebay. These tracks depicted the movement behavior of multiple species (in three dimensions) during different diel periods, spill conditions, powerhouse operations, and test configurations of the TSWs. One of the challenges in reporting 3-D results is presenting the information in a manner that allows interested parties to summarize the behavior of many fish over many different conditions across multiple years. To help facilitate this, the U.S. Geological Survey (USGS) worked with a software development company (Myriax Software Pty Ltd., Hobart, Tasmania, Australia) in 2010 to produce a software interface (Eonfusion™) to allow users to query the data, summarize it across multiple species and conditions, and visualize the fish movement tracks in a 3-D format. The USGS continued to refine the software interface in 2011. Although the initial software provides an excellent way to summarize and visualize 3-D data, it is still a relatively complex task and needs to be simplified so interested parties are more likely to take advantage of this powerful tool.

Even with the refinement of the software interface, it will only summarize, not analyze, the 3-D movement information. For example, the software interface will allow the user to visually examine all of the fish movement tracks for all fish that approached the spillway during the night, but does not have the capacity to numerically analyze the data. The software lacks the ability to quantify the inherently qualitative nature of the fish movement tracks. To accomplish this, we investigated the feasibility of using a Markov chain analysis to numerically characterize fish movement patterns in the forebay of McNary Dam (Steel and others, 2001; Johnson and others, 2004).

Markov Chain Methods

A Markov chain is a stochastic process that specifies the probability of transitioning from one state to another (Stewart and Stewart, 1994). States, in this case, were six discrete areas across the face of the dam, which consisted of 3-D volumes of water bounded by the water surface and the river bottom, and extended from the face of the dam upstream 60 m (fig. 1). Within each state, fish could either pass the dam or swim to an adjoining state (fig. 2). A fish was said to have been absorbed within the state if it passes the dam, and the term "transition" is used to describe movement from one state to another. The transition history of individual fish movements between states was used to construct a transition matrix and includes all fish movement information within 60 m of the upstream face of McNary Dam. Because fish swam back and forth upstream of the dam, individual fish were counted multiple times within each state. For instance, a single fish may have entered and exited the same state multiple times before it was absorbed in any particular state. As a result, it was possible to have, for example, 100 transitions from state Y to state Z that were based on the movements of 10 individual fish that traveled from state Y to state Z on 10 separate occasions. Equally plausible is that 100 individual fish each moved only once between state Y and Z. The transition matrix was then used to calculate the probability of fish movement from one state to the next for all six states upstream of McNary Dam.

The probability of moving from one state to another is assumed to be independent of which state the fish was in previously. Therefore, transitioning out of any given state is not dependent on which state the fish was in previously. This is the primary assumption of a one-step Markov chain analysis. To investigate how the transitions from one state depended on which state the fish was in previously, we also constructed a two-step analysis. The two-step analysis examined the transitions of fish in state Y as a function of which state they were in previously. For example, if state X, Y, and Z represented adjoining states located across the upstream face of the dam, we examined the transitions of fish out of state Y that had moved into Y from X, as well as the transitions of fish out of state Y that had moved into Y from state Z. Both the one-step and two-step analyses allowed us to investigate and quantify the movement behavior of fish upstream of McNary Dam.

Figure 1. Graphical representation of the upstream face of McNary Dam showing the powerhouse (left) and spillway (right). The vertical purple lines indicate how the area upstream (within 60 m) of the dam was partitioned into six areas for the Markov chain analysis.

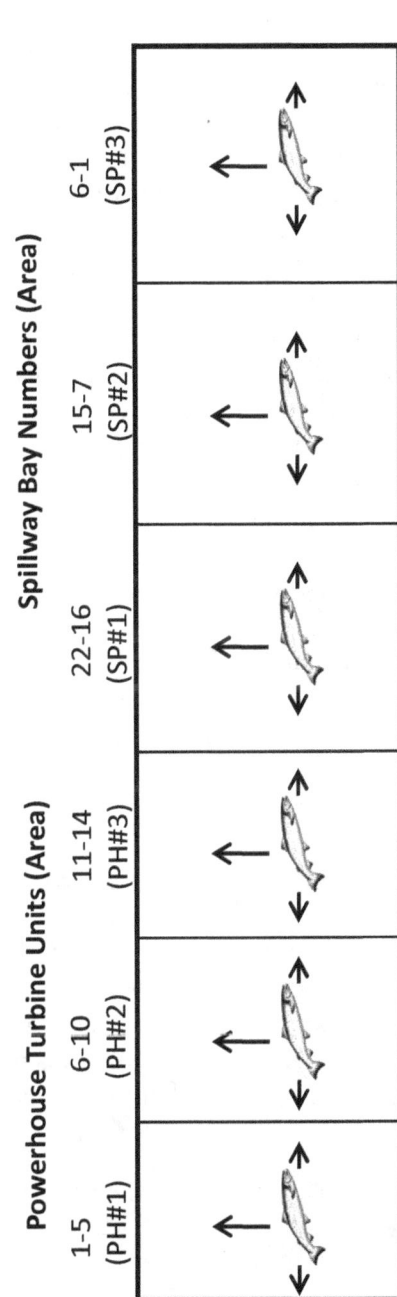

Figure 2. Diagram showing a top view of the three powerhouse and three spillway areas upstream of McNary Dam used in the Markov chain analysis. Within each area, the one-step analysis examined the probability of fish passing the dam or transitioning to an adjoining area. The two-step analysis examined the probability of a fish passing the dam or transitioning to an adjoining area as a function of the area it was in previously.

Environmental and Biological Setting

Project Description

McNary Dam is the fourth dam upstream of the mouth of the Columbia River, located 470 river kilometers (rkm) upstream of the Pacific Ocean and 52 rkm downstream of the confluence of the Columbia and Snake Rivers. The reservoir formed by McNary Dam (Lake Wallula) extends 98 rkm upstream to the Hanford Reach on the Columbia River, and impounds 16 rkm of the Snake River upstream to Ice Harbor Dam. The river downstream of McNary Dam (Lake Umatilla) is impounded by John Day Dam located 123 rkm downstream of McNary Dam. The study area encompassed 482 km, extending from the tailrace of Wells Dam (rkm 830), the upper most release point for tagged fish, to our most downstream detection array located at John Day Dam (rkm 348) (fig. 3).

McNary Dam is oriented perpendicular to the river channel with a navigation lock, spillway, powerhouse, and earthen dam. The spillway is 399 m long with 22 vertical lift-type spill gates that regulate discharge through the dam. The spillway discharges water at the ogee crest approximately 14 m below the water surface. The powerhouse at McNary Dam is 433 m long with 14 turbine units. Each turbine unit has a generating capacity of 70 megawatts and a hydraulic capacity of 16.6 kcfs (thousand cubic feet per second, or 1,000 ft³/s). The turbine intakes are about 19 m deep, and are divided into three smaller, fully isolated slots. Each slot has a vertical barrier screen, trash rack (designed to prevent large debris from entering the turbines), and an extended-length submersible barrier screen that guides downstream migrating fish away from the turbine intakes and into the fish collection channel (orifice gallery). These fish are then guided through a series of pipes and channels to the juvenile fish bypass facility and held in concrete raceways where they await downstream transportation by barge or truck, or are routed back into the river to continue their migration. Some fish in the Federal Columbia River Power System are implanted with passive integrated transponder (PIT) tags to identify the fish's route of passage through the dams encountered during its migration. In addition to the acoustic tag, we also implanted PIT tags in our study fish. Because PIT-tagged fish were detected passing through the McNary Dam bypass system, we were able to distinguish bypass passage from turbine passage. No study fish with PIT tags were barged during our years of study. This ensured that our study fish were kept in the river to enable detection at receivers downstream of McNary Dam.

Two TSW designs were tested during 2007, 2008, and 2009 (fig. 4). Different locations were tested for TSW design 1 during the study years to determine if TSW location affected fish passage or survival. TSW design 1 was installed in spill bay 22 during 2007, spill bay 19 during 2008, spill bay 4 during spring of 2009, and spill bay 19 during summer of 2009 (fig. 5). TSW design 2 was installed in spill bay 20 during all three study years. Each TSW was comprised of a weir crest, set atop the spill leaf gate within the spill bay. The weir crest extended from the top of the ogee crest to about 2.4 m below the surface, thereby causing water to spill from the surface of the forebay rather than from 14 m below the surface like conventional spill bays. Discharge over the TSWs was a function of forebay elevation, and because TSW design 1 was about 0.2 m deeper than TSW design 2, discharge through TSW design 1 was, on average, slightly greater (about 600 ft³/s) than discharge through TSW design 2. The difference in the elevation of the TSWs was the result of structural differences (fig. 4) to test the efficacy of varying entrance conditions for passing juvenile salmonids.

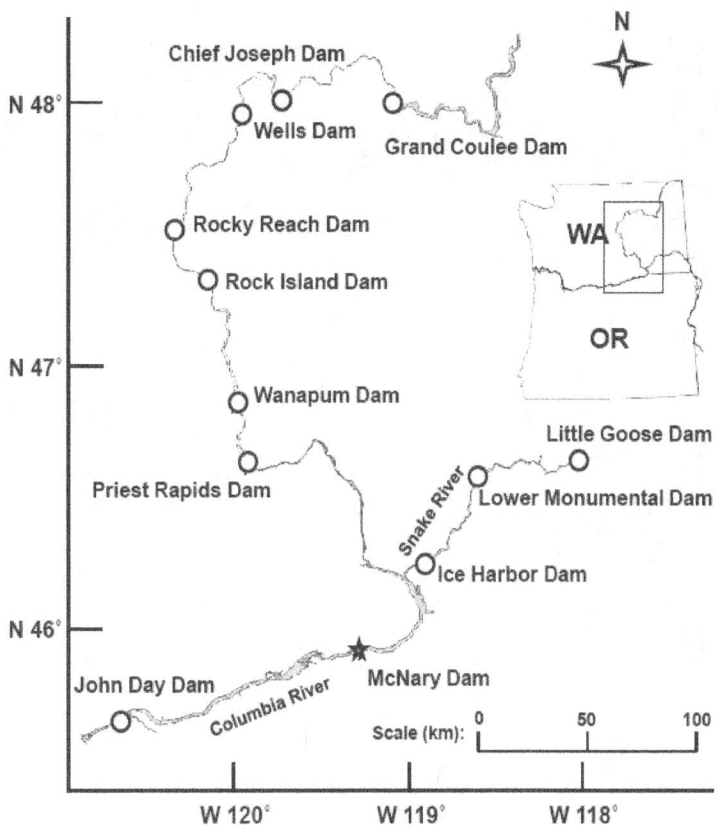

Figure 3. Map showing Columbia and Snake Rivers and the location of McNary Dam relative to other major hydroelectric projects in the region.

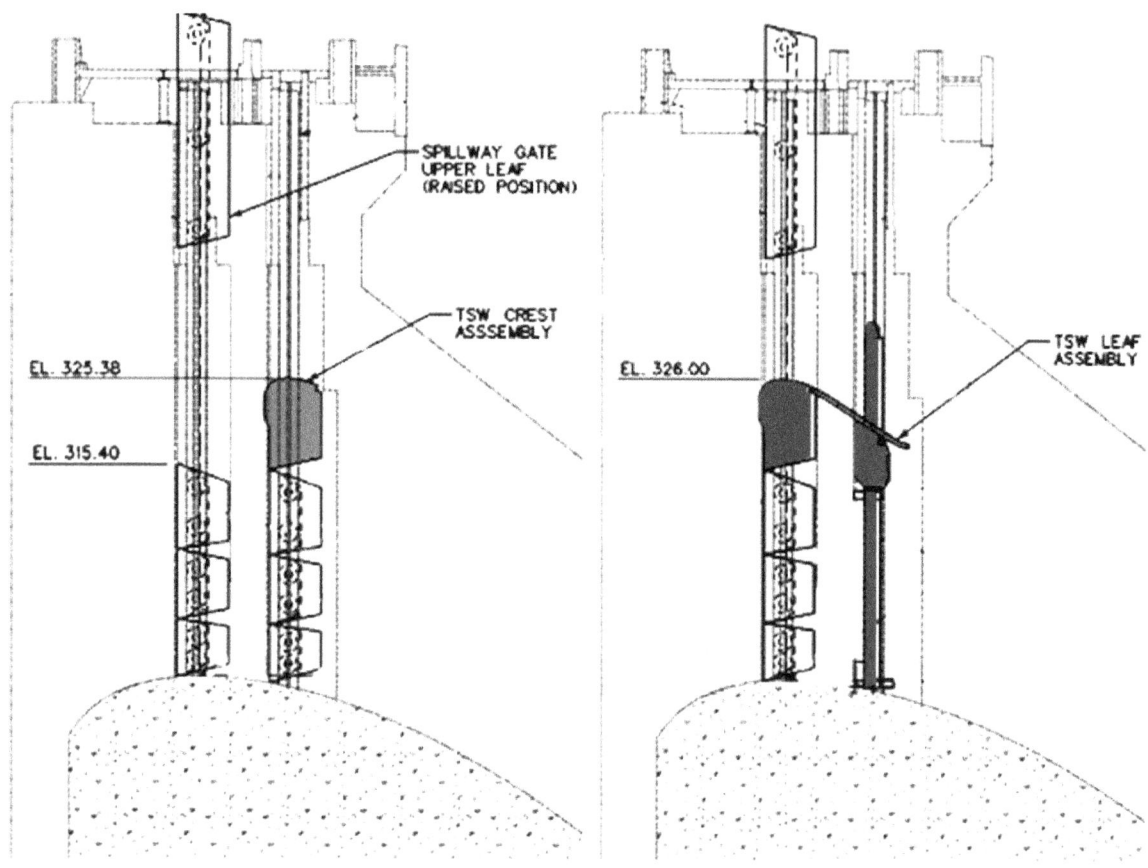

Figure 4. Cross-sectional view of the spillway at McNary Dam showing temporary spillway weir (TSW) (gray shaded area) design 1 (left diagram) and design 2 (right diagram). Water spilled over the TSW crest from the forebay (left side of page) to the tailrace (right side of page).

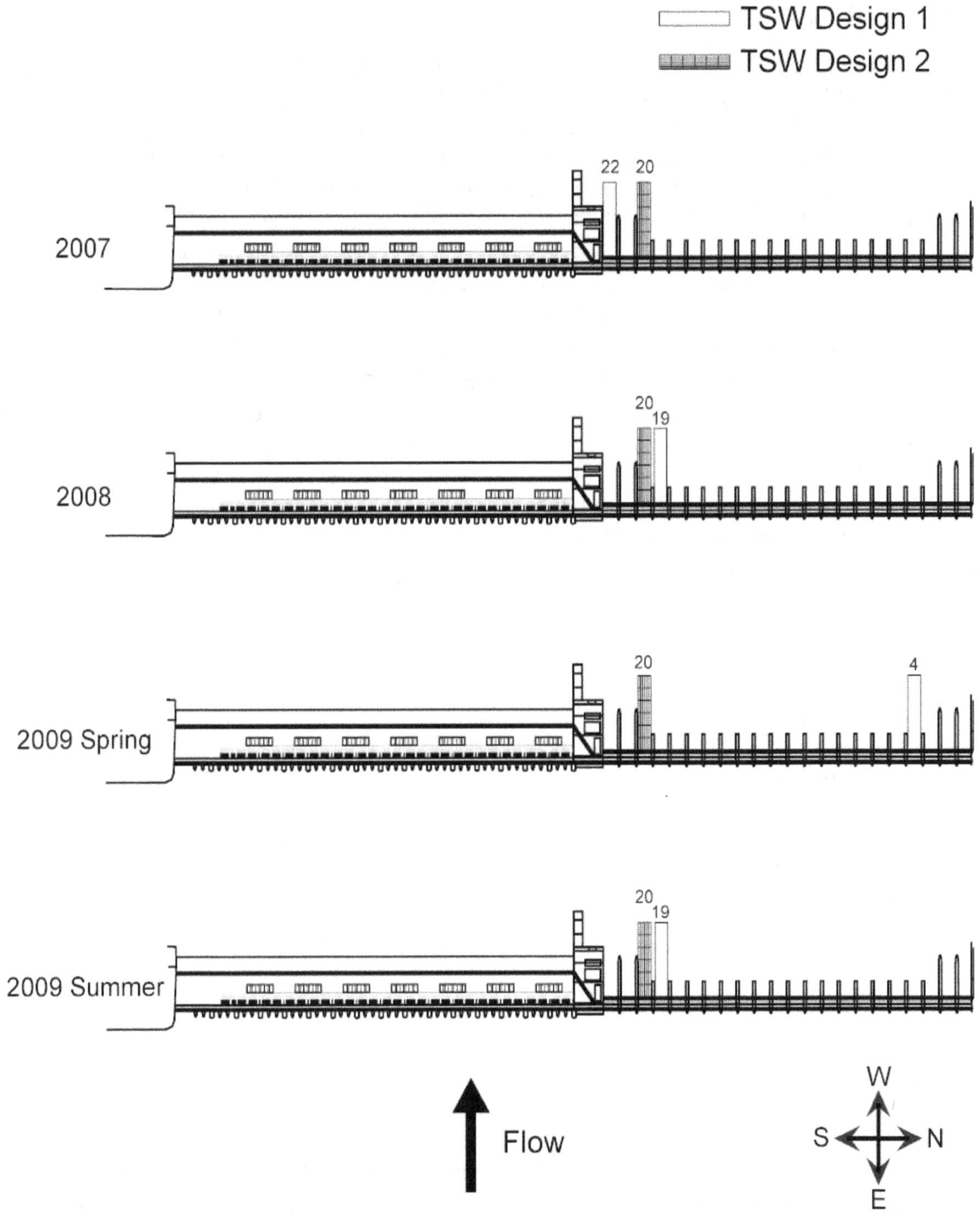

TSW Design 1
TSW Design 2

2007

22 20

2008

20
19

2009 Spring

20

4

2009 Summer

20
19

Flow

W
S — N
E

Figure 5. Plan view of McNary Dam showing locations of temporary spillway weirs (TSWs) in 2007, 2008, and 2009. Numbers above the TSW icon indicate spill bay number. There were no TSWs in 2006.

River Conditions

Mean daily discharge at McNary Dam throughout our study seasons was variable, depending upon year, but was similar to the 10-year average (2000–09) (fig. 6). The 10-year average discharge in mid-April was about 210 kcfs, increasing above 250 kcfs by late May, decreasing through June and July, and ending below 150 kcfs by August. Our study years followed a similar trend but were more pronounced, depending on the year. During the spring study dates, the median daily project outflow was ranked highest in 2006, 2009, and 2008, respectively, and 2007 ranked fifth of the 10-year average. During the summer study dates, 2008 and 2006 were ranked second and third highest, and 2007 and 2009 ranked fifth and sixth for median daily project outflow.

Mean daily spill at McNary Dam from 2000 to 2009 followed a similar trend to mean daily discharge (fig. 7). Mean daily spill in mid-April, at the start of the season, averaged 80 kcfs and peaked in late May or early June at 125 kcfs for the 10-year average. In 2008, the average daily maximum spill was 250 kcfs. Daily spill typically was lowest in July, near the end of the study period, at an average of 50 kcfs.

Water temperature steadily increased during the study period, rising from 9° C in April to a peak of about 21° C in late July or early August (fig. 8). Water temperatures were slightly lower (1–2° C) in 2008 than in the other three study years.

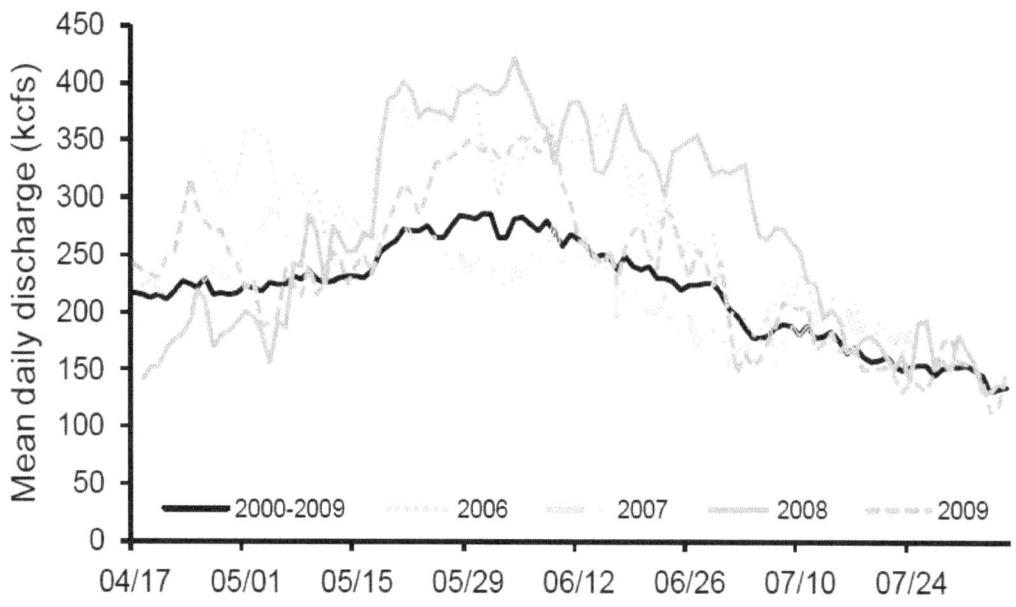

Figure 6. Hydrograph of mean daily project outflow (in kcfs, thousands of cubic feet per second) during acoustic telemetry study dates at McNary Dam, 2006–09, and the 10-year average, 2000–09. Data obtained from Columbia River DART website: *http://www.cbr.washington.edu/dart/river.html*

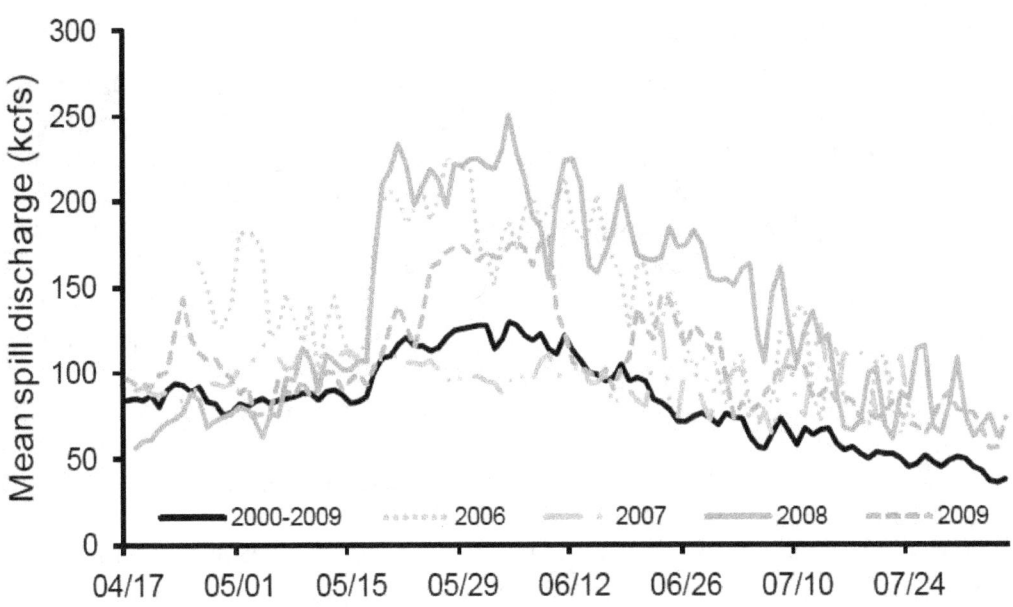

Figure 7. Hydrograph of mean daily project spill (in kcfs, thousands of cubic feet per second) during acoustic telemetry study dates at McNary Dam, 2006–09, and the 10-year average, 2000–09. Data obtained from Columbia River DART website: *http://www.cbr.washington.edu/dart/river.html*

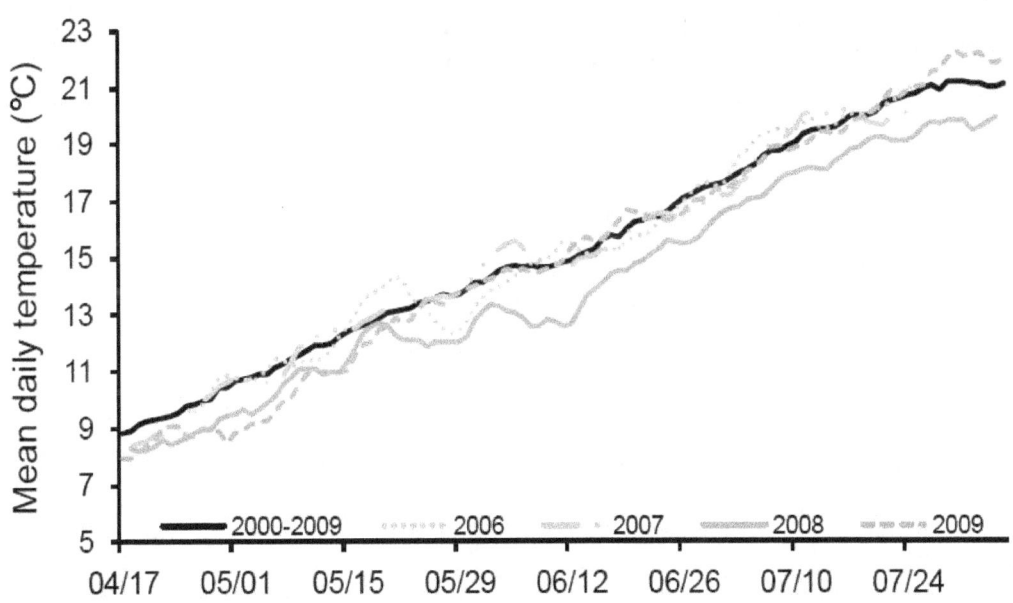

Figure 8. Hydrograph of mean daily water temperature [in degrees Celsius (C)] of the Columbia River at McNary Dam during acoustic telemetry study dates, 2006–09, and the 10-year average, 2000–09. Data obtained from Columbia River DART website: *http://www.cbr.washington.edu/dart/river.html*.

Project Operations and Study Treatments

Several treatments and operation schemes were implemented at McNary Dam between 2006 and 2009 (table 1; figs. 9 and 10). Two treatments (Fish Passage Plan and 2006 Test Spill) were conducted during spring 2006. The Fish Passage Plan treatment consisted of high discharge at the northern end of the spillway. Conversely, the 2006 Test Spill pattern consisted of high discharge at the southern end of the spillway. During spring 2007, the two treatments were a modification of the 2006 Test Spill (hereafter called Modified 2006 Test Spill) and a 2007 Test Spill pattern. Investigations into dam operations based on this schedule, however, revealed few differences between the spill treatments. Differences in spill bay- and turbine-specific discharge primarily were associated with spill bays 15, 16, and 17 (fig. 9) No treatments were planned in spring 2008 or 2009; however, we characterized two treatments in 2008. During the first one-half of the spring season (April 18–May 17), discharge through the spillway was 40 percent, hereafter called Early Season. During the second one-half of the season (May 17–June 9), spillway discharge was 50–60 percent, hereafter called Late Season. We were unable to characterize any spill patterns in 2009.

Two treatment types were tested during the summer seasons between 2006 and 2009 (fig. 10). For the 2006 and 2007 treatments, two dam operations were evaluated: 24-hour (h) spill at 40 percent of total river discharge and 24-h spill at 60 percent of total river discharge. Sixty percent spill and 40 percent spill also were planned and implemented in 2008 in randomized 4-day (d) blocks; however, the treatments began after July 3. Prior to July 3, high dissolved gas levels and involuntary spill prevented operation at the treatment level. The period of time before July 3 is hereafter called Early Season, which consisted of approximately 50 percent spill of total project discharge. No treatments were planned or characterized in summer 2009. For both spring and summer, diel periods were assigned as day (0600–1759 hours) and night (1800–0559 hours). Additional information about project operations and treatments can be found in the annual reports of research (Adams and Counihan, 2009; Adams and Liedtke, 2010; and Adams and Evans, 2011).

Table 1. Summary of study dates, seasonal treatment types, and seasonal mean daily project discharge for acoustic telemetry studies at McNary Dam, 2006–09.

[Discharge is measured in thousand ft^3/s. Abbreviations: %, percent; NA, not applicable]

	2006	2007	2008	2009
Spring study dates	Apr 26–June 07	Apr 18–June 06	Apr 18–June 09	Apr 17–June 10
Spring Treatments[1]	Fish Passage Plan	Modified 2006 test spill	Early season (40% spill)	NA
	2006 test spill	2007 test spill	Late season (50–60% spill)	NA
Mean project discharge	334.6	251.7	283.6	278.5
TSW Design 1 location	NA	Spill bay 22	Spill bay 19	Spill bay 4
TSW Design 2 location	NA	Spill bay 20	Spill bay 20	Spill bay 20
Summer study dates	Jun 19–Jul 25	Jun 20–Jul 26	Jun 18–Aug 04	Jun 19–Aug 05
Summer Treatments[1]	60% spill	60% spill	Early season (~50% spill)	NA
	40% spill	40% spill	60% spill	NA
	NA	NA	40% spill	NA
Mean project discharge	219.2	184.0	241.0	184.9
TSW Design 1 location	NA	Spill bay 22	Spill bay 19	Spill bay 19[2]
TSW Design 2 location	NA	Spill bay 20	Spill bay 20	Spill bay 20

[1]Treatments represent spill patterns proposed by regional fishery managers. Although no treatments were proposed for 2008, we characterized treatments based on distinct spill patterns that occurred. No treatments were proposed for 2009 and none were characterized.

[2]TSW Design 1 was moved to spill bay 19 for the 2009 summer study, but passage could be calculated only for spill bays 16–19 as a group because the necessary monitoring equipment was not in place that would allow specific-bay passage.

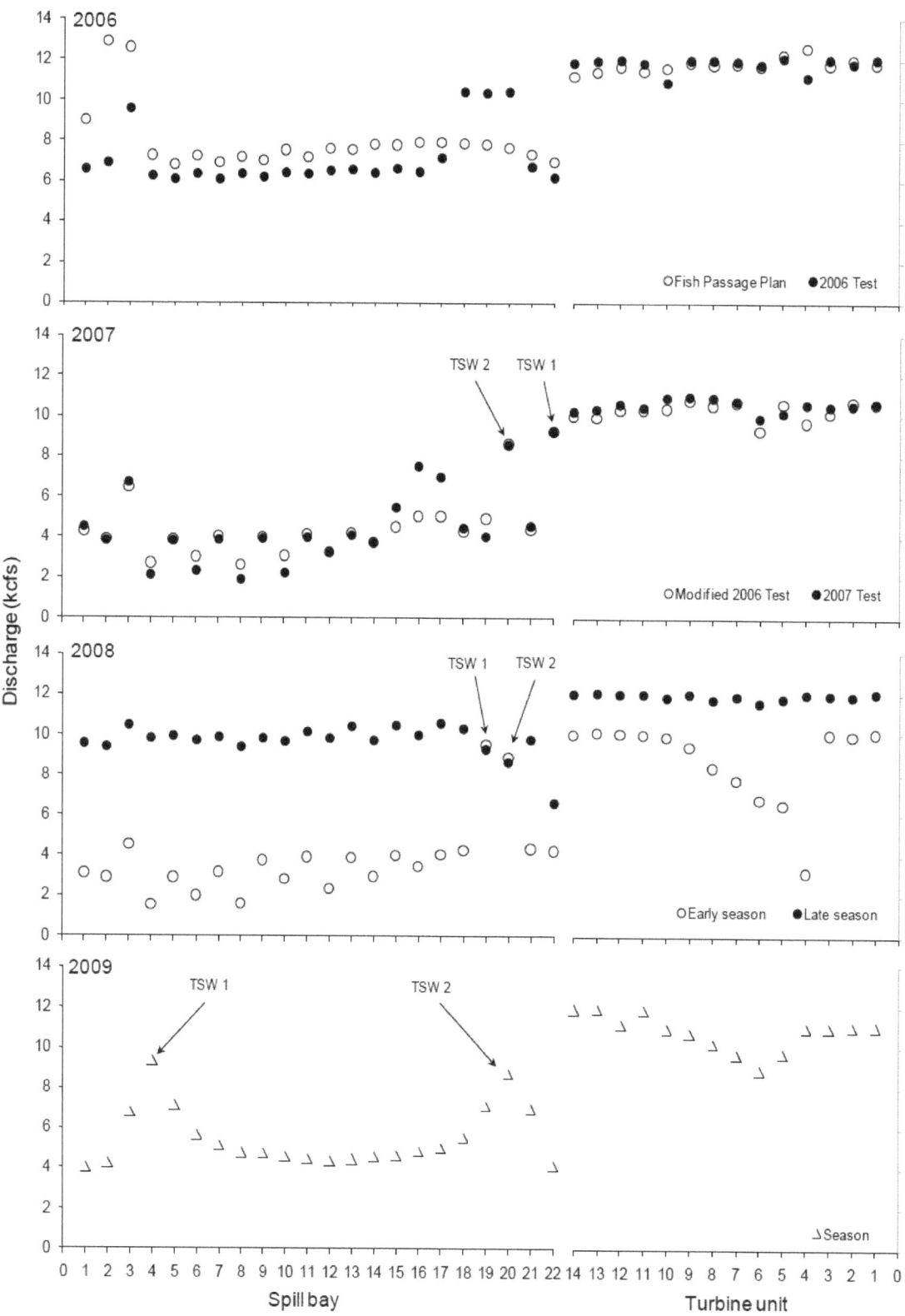

Figure 9. Graphs showing mean discharge (in kcfs, thousands of cubic feet per second) of spill bays and turbine units by treatments or conditions during spring acoustic telemetry studies at McNary Dam, 2006–09.

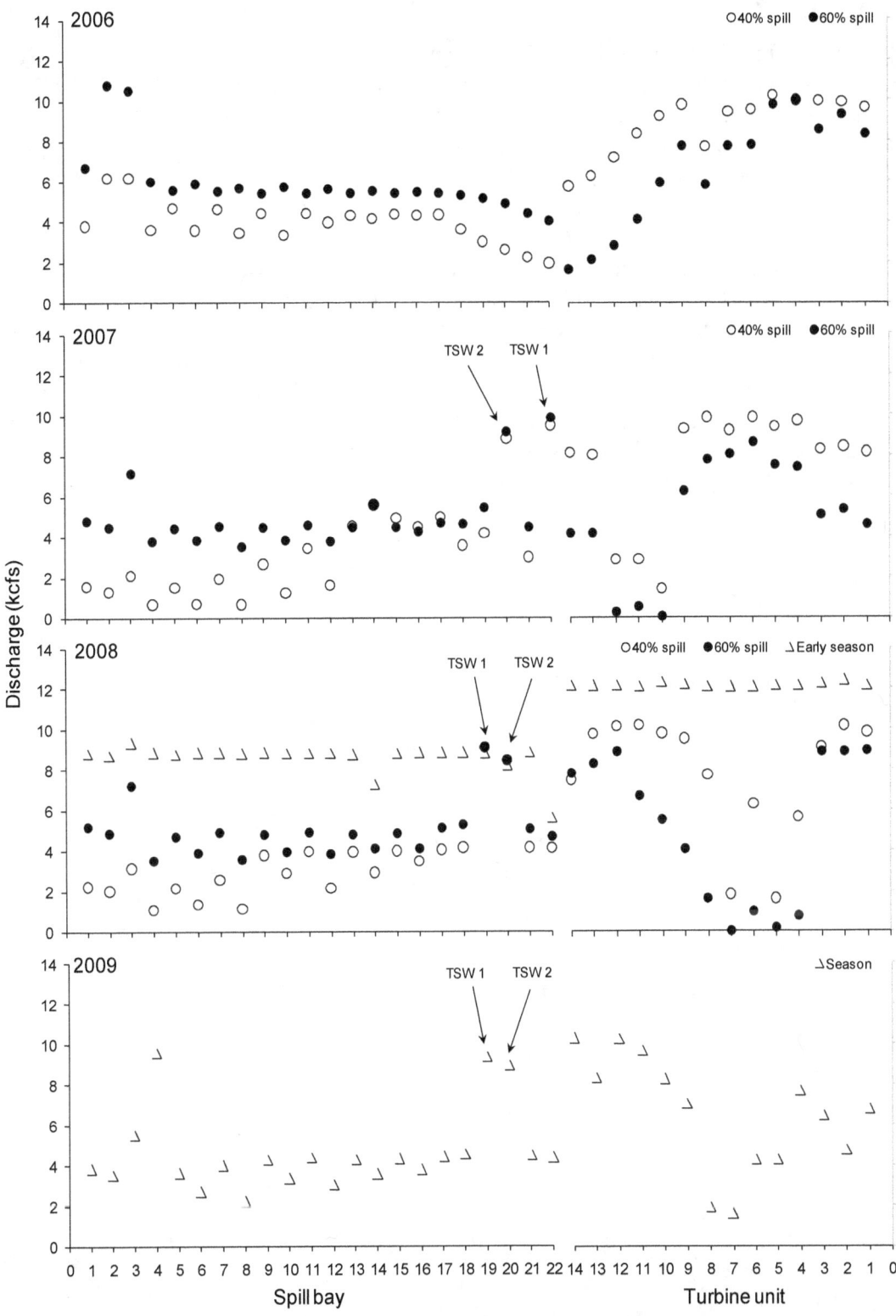

Figure 10. Graphs showing mean discharge (in kcfs, thousands of cubic feet per second) of spill bays and turbine units by treatments or conditions during summer acoustic telemetry studies at McNary Dam, 2006–09.

Species Composition and Run Timing

Run timing from 2006 to 2009 at McNary Dam varied by species and year and generally followed the 10-year average in pattern but not in scale. During the spring, juvenile yearling Chinook salmon (*Oncorhynchus tshawytscha)*, coho salmon (*O. kisutch*), sockeye salmon (*O. nerka*), and steelhead (*O. mykiss*) made up the majority of the fish run, but yearling Chinook salmon and juvenile steelhead were the most prevalent (fig. 11). Subyearling Chinook salmon made up the greatest proportion of the fish run during the summer study periods as well as over the entire 4-year study period (0.566; table 2).

Across years, numbers of sockeye and subyearling Chinook salmon passing McNary Dam were greatest in 2007, numbers of yearling Chinook salmon and juvenile steelhead passing McNary Dam were greatest in 2009, and the number of coho salmon passing McNary Dam was greatest in 2008. Most fish runs that passed McNary Dam in the spring from 2006 to 2009 had higher daily counts than the 10-year average. Only numbers of subyearling Chinook salmon during 2006–09 was consistent with the 10-year average, but the peak of the run during 2006–09 peaked several weeks later than the 10-year average. Additional information about species composition and run timing can be found in the annual reports of research (Adams and Counihan, 2009; Adams and Liedtke, 2010; and Adams and Evans, 2011).

Table 2. Mean numbers of juvenile fish passing McNary Dam between April 1 and December 1 by year and species.

[Proportion is the total number of each species divided by all fish passing McNary Dam (2006–09). Data obtained from the Fish Passage Center (*http://www.fpc.org*)]

Species	2006	2007	2008	2009	Total	Proportion
Yearling Chinook salmon	1,559,649	2,223,432	1,299,990	2,249,069	7,332,140	0.280
Coho	102,125	99,101	168,497	127,002	496,725	0.019
Sockeye	496,470	512,994	221,747	190,747	1,421,958	0.054
Steelhead	442,984	376,449	506,527	803,445	2,129,405	0.081
Subyearling Chinook salmon	4,064,681	4,721,057	2,408,207	3,652,430	14,846,375	0.566
Total	6,665,909	7,933,033	4,604,968	7,022,693	26,226,603	

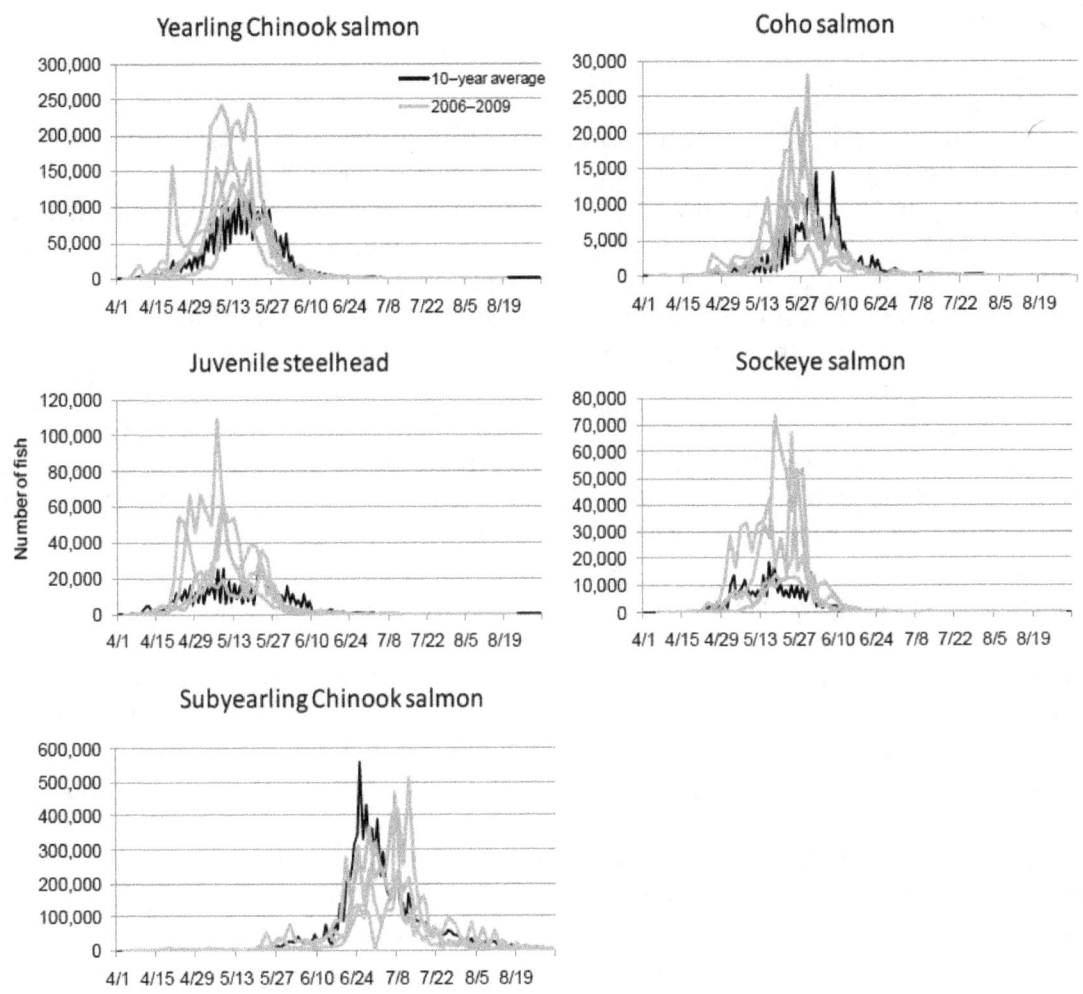

Figure 11. Numbers of juvenile salmonids (yearling Chinook salmon, coho salmon, juvenile steelhead, sockeye salmon, and subyearling Chinook salmon) passing McNary Dam in relation to date. Lines represent the 10-year average (black line) and annual numbers for 2006–09 (gray lines). Data obtained from the Fish Passage Center (*http://www.fpc.org*).

Study Design

Acoustic Telemetry System

The acoustic telemetry system used to track fish consisted of acoustic receivers, hydrophones, and transmitters (tags). All hydrophones (model 590; Hydroacoustic Technology, Inc., HTI[©]; Seattle, Wash.) had a 290° beam width and were monitored continuously by either an acoustic telemetry receiver (ATR) (model 290; HTI[©]) or an acoustic tag data logger (ATDL) (model 295-X; HTI[©]).

The number and layout of hydrophones varied throughout the study years because of attempts to improve 3-D coverage from year to year, movement of TSWs, or other changes in objectives. Depending on the year of study, 86–113 hydrophones were linked to 5–7 ATRs and 17–20 ATDLs. In the forebay, hydrophones were mounted about 2 m below the water surface and near the bottom (greater than 18.3 m below the surface) of the river. Double hydrophone arrays were installed at all dam passage routes to permit the estimation of route-specific detection probabilities and use of the route-specific survival model (Skalski and others, 2002). At remote detection arrays located upstream and downstream of the dam, hydrophones were deployed on floating barges or pre-existing structures (for example, bridge pilings, navigation markers, and navigation walls) at depths of 1.5 to 2.1 m, depending on the location. At locations where surface-mounting was not feasible, hydrophones were deployed about 1 m above the river bottom using steel towers. Satellite or cellular modems were deployed at each hydrophone array to establish a wireless network between each ATDL or ATR, and our data processing servers at the Columbia River Research Laboratory. This network allowed automated transfer of data, as well as the ability to access and control each ATDL and ATR remotely. More detailed descriptions of hydrophone arrays are provided in Adams and others (2008), Adams and Counihan (2009), and Adams and Liedtke (2009, 2010).

Although the same manufacturer and models of acoustic telemetry receiving equipment were used during all study years, and hydrophones were mounted to detect fish passing through any route, there were differences in system deployment among years. These differences were caused by changing locations of the TSWs, changing objectives, or improving the detection performance of the hydrophones by locating them away from sources of noise. Appendix A portrays the different layouts of our telemetry systems from year to year. Some changes in deployment are not distinguishable on the plan views. One example includes the mounting of hydrophones 3 m lower on the spillway pier noses in 2007, 2008, and 2009 (compared to 2006) to decrease noise induced by flow at the spillway ogee. An example that is distinguishable in appendix A includes the different location of deep hydrophones at the powerhouse in 2009, compared to other years. In 2009, we deployed deep hydrophones on towers located 60 m in front of the powerhouse on the forebay floor, rather than using divers to mount the hydrophones directly to the powerhouse on the pier noses. This change was implemented at the request of the U.S. Army Corps of Engineers to reduce installation costs. The change also reduced the amount of noise detected by the monitoring system, thereby improving system performance. Additional information about differences in the monitoring system across years can be found in the annual reports of research (Adams and Counihan, 2009; Adams and Leidtke, 2010; and Adams and Evans, 2011).

Transmitters

We used acoustic transmitters that operated at a frequency of 307.5 kHz with a 1.0–2.0 ms pulse width. Transmitter size and weight varied depending on the year of study and model of tag used (table 3). Each transmitter emitted a unique acoustic signal (encoded by pulse rate), allowing simultaneous monitoring of multiple transmitters by a single hydrophone. In addition to the acoustic transmitter, we inserted a PIT-tag (Destron-Fearing™ model TX1411ST) into each fish to enable determination of fish passage through the juvenile fish bypass system at McNary Dam. Each PIT-tag emitted a unique digitally-encoded signal at 134.2 kHz when activated by an electromagnetic field from a PIT-tag detector. Each PIT-tag weighed about 0.1 g in air. The additional weight and volume from the PIT-tag added a negligible amount of weight and volume to the fish relative to the acoustic transmitter.

Studies of the lifespan of acoustic tags were conducted by USGS in 2006, 2007, 2008, and 2009 (Adams and others, 2008; Adams and Counihan, 2009; Adams and Liedtke, 2009, 2010). These studies indicated the average lifespan was between 18 and 28 d for tags implanted in juvenile steelhead and yearling Chinook salmon and between 13 and 24 d for tags implanted in subyearling Chinook salmon, depending on tag model and year (table 3).

Table 3. Specifications of transmitters surgically implanted in juvenile salmonids, 2006–09.

Year	Acoustic transmitter model	Average tag dimensions (millimeters)	Average tag weight in air (grams)	Average tag life (days)
Yearling Chinook salmon and juvenile steelhead				
2006	795-E	6.8 × 21.0	1.5	21
2007	795-E	6.8 × 21.0	1.5	21
2008	795-E	7.1 × 21.9	1.6	18
2009	795-LE	6.7 × 21.1	1.4	28
Subyearling Chinook salmon				
2006	795-M	6.8 × 16.5	0.8	17
2007	795-M	6.8 × 16.5	0.8	17
2008	795-S	6.5 × 22.2	0.7	13
2009	795-LM	6.5 × 16.3	0.7	24

Fish Tagging and Release

All fish were tagged and released by personnel from USGS using methodology and protocols described by Adams and others (1998). The source, collection, and release sites for each species and release group are briefly documented in this report but detailed descriptions of collection, transport, and tagging procedures can be found in Adams and others (2008), Adams and Counihan (2009), and Adams and Liedtke (2009, 2010). Yearling and subyearling Chinook salmon and juvenile steelhead were collected, tagged, and held at the McNary Dam smolt monitoring facility operated by the Washington Department of Fish and Wildlife. For all experimental groups, handling protocols (regarding collection, transport, tagging, holding, and release) were standardized as much as possible among release groups to reduce the potential for bias arising from differences in handling methods and time. All acoustic transmitters were surgically implanted. Fish were held for 18–36 h before and after tagging to minimize stress associated with handling. The treatment release location was approximately 10 rkm upstream of McNary Dam at Hat Rock State Park, Oregon; a distance upstream of the dam considered sufficient for allowing fish to mix naturally in the river before reaching the dam. Control groups were released in the tailrace of McNary Dam, directly out from the downstream tip of the navigation wall. Both treatment and control groups were released across the main channel in three locations (north, middle, and south of main river channel) to allow greater distribution in the river. To distribute fish arrival times at the dam, we released fish throughout the 24-h diel cycle. Species, release dates, release sites, passage dates, and percent spill during dates of passage are documented in tables 4 and 5.

Signal Processing and Verification

Passage routes, approach distributions, and travel times were determined from acoustic transmitter signals collected by hydrophones at the dam and in the reservoir. Valid acoustic signals were separated from ambient noise using the HTI[©] MarkTags software. Files were then compiled and the auto-marking software identified individual tags to be verified by data technicians. Tracking parameters were set in the software to minimize the marking of false detections caused by noise or overlap of individual tags and to maximize detections of available fish (based on a tag list of all possible tags). Tag lists were generated for each batch based on a search duration determined by the estimated travel time information. Once fish records were verified by technicians, a second round of processing occurred with a wider parameter set and search duration and a smaller tag list to look for remaining undetected fish. All verified fish records were then compiled and detections of individual fish were identified and given to data technicians for manual marking of the individual tracks. After manual marking, the MarkTags software was used to assign a date and time for the beginning and end of each valid acoustic track. The detections were then used to estimate the proximity of an acoustic transmitter to hydrophones in the array and to estimate the 2-D and 3-D locations of the acoustic transmitters.

Table 4. Summary statistics of fork length and weight of acoustic-tagged juvenile salmonids released in the Columbia River by release site, 2006–09.

[Species: Y. Chinook, yearling Chinook salmon; Steelhead, juvenile steelhead; S. Chinook, subyearling Chinook salmon. Release site: HAT, Near Hat Rock State Park, Oregon, approximately 10 km upstream of McNary Dam; TAIL, 0.5 km downstream of McNary Dam in the tailrace directly out from the downstream tip of the navigation wall; SAC, intentionally sacrificed fish released at the TAIL release site. N, number of fish; Min, minimum; Max, maximum]

Species/ age class	Release site	Release dates	N	Fork length, in millimeters			Weight, in grams		
				Mean	Min	Max	Mean	Min	Max
2006									
Y. Chinook	HAT	4/27–6/4	1,797	149	125	179	31.7	23.0	59.5
Y. Chinook	TAIL	4/27–6/4	1,213	148	133	175	31.3	22.6	49.8
Y. Chinook	SAC	4/30–6/1	49	148	134	174	31.7	23.0	48.7
Steelhead	HAT	4/27–6/1	1,005	209	122	290	78.6	31.0	236.5
Steelhead	SAC	5/4–5/31	50	205	158	267	73.3	30.1	152.6
S. Chinook	HAT	6/20–7/19	1,794	120	104	155	17.5	12.5	44.8
S. Chinook	TAIL	6/20–7/19	1,191	120	108	158	17.4	13.5	44.9
S. Chinook	SAC	6/22–7/11	50	118	112	133	16.7	13.6	25.1
2007									
Y. Chinook	HAT	4/19–6/7	1,973	151	130	222	33.4	23.0	108.4
Y. Chinook	TAIL	4/19–6/7	1,310	151	133	206	33.5	23.0	78.8
Y. Chinook	SAC	4/27–6/4	53	151	135	179	33.2	23.7	49.9
Steelhead	HAT	4/21–6/6	1,118	215	160	292	84.6	27.4	207.7
Steelhead	SAC	4/28–6/2	50	223	178	279	93.4	43.7	166.8
S. Chinook	HAT	6/20–7/25	1,771	118	105	166	17.8	13.2	55.2
S. Chinook	TAIL	6/20–7/25	1,182	118	105	168	17.6	12.8	59.9
S. Chinook	SAC	6/24–7/24	50	118	110	136	17.8	13.5	32.5
2008									
Y. Chinook	HAT	4/19–6/3	1,424	154	131	206	36.0	23.0	147.6
Y. Chinook	TAIL	4/20–6/4	949	153	130	200	35.5	23.0	76.7
Y. Chinook	SAC	4/22–5/31	50	151	134	189	34.2	24.1	63.6
Steelhead	HAT	4/19–6/2	1,186	211	136	289	82.8	27.5	224.0
Steelhead	TAIL	4/20–6/3	785	210	135	294	81.7	25.0	232.7
Steelhead	SAC	4/22–5/31	50	213	171	270	87.2	38.3	179.2
S. Chinook	HAT	6/19–7/28	1,752	116	102	158	17.1	11.8	46.8
S. Chinook	TAIL	6/20–7/29	1,176	117	103	155	17.1	11.8	40.7
S. Chinook	SAC	6/22–7/27	50	117	107	142	17.4	12.4	33.3
2009									
Y. Chinook	HAT	4/18–6/4	1,411	164	134	240	44.4	29.0	119.0
Y. Chinook	TAIL	4/18–6/4	935	164	137	255	44.7	29.0	174.0
Y. Chinook	SAC	4/20–5/29	51	161	143	195	41.9	30.4	75.2
Steelhead	HAT	4/18–6/4	1,176	220	111	280	93.8	32.6	215.4
Steelhead	TAIL	4/18–6/4	785	220	158	283	94.7	32.4	218.0
Steelhead	SAC	4/23–5/29	51	216	156	254	87.4	31.5	130.0
S. Chinook	HAT	6/20–7/30	1,784	121	105	158	20.2	13.5	47.0
S. Chinook	TAIL	6/20–7/30	1,187	122	102	172	20.4	13.5	57.8
S. Chinook	SAC	6/25–7/28	51	118	109	148	18.8	14.0	38.2

Table 5. Number of acoustic-tagged juvenile salmonids released in the Columbia River, number (and percentage of those released) that passed McNary Dam, range of passage dates, and corresponding percentage of spill of total project discharge over dates of passage at McNary Dam, by species, 2006–09.

[Y. Chinook, yearling Chinook salmon; Steelhead, juvenile steelhead; S. Chinook, subyearling Chinook salmon]

Species/ age class	Number released	Number passed (percentage)	First passage date	Last passage date	Percent spill[1]
2006					
Y. Chinook	1,797	1,717 (96)	4/27/2006	6/5/2006	50
Steelhead	1,005	944 (94)	4/27/2006	6/2/2006	48
S. Chinook	1,791	1,638 (91)	6/20/2006	7/30/2006	49
2007					
Y. Chinook	1,974	1,911 (97)	4/20/2007	6/9/2007	43
Steelhead	1,118	1,086 (97)	4/22/2007	6/9/2007	41
S. Chinook	1,771	1,631 (92)	6/21/2007	8/7/2007	52
2008					
Y. Chinook	1,424	1,396 (98)	4/19/2008	6/8/2008	46
Steelhead	1,186	1,186 (100)	4/19/2008	6/3/2008	47
S. Chinook	1,752	1,646 (94)	6/20/2008	8/8/2008	51
2009					
Y. Chinook	1,403	1,351 (96)	4/18/2009	6/8/2009	44
Steelhead	1,170	1,107 (95)	4/19/2009	6/4/2009	43
S. Chinook	1,772	1,602 (90)	6/20/2009	8/7/2009	51

[1]The percentage of project discharge spilled includes the water discharged through the temporary spillway weirs.

Results

Results from the one-step Markov analysis will be presented first, followed by results from the two-step analysis. Within these sections, results will be presented for all fish regardless of where they first approached the dam, followed by all fish that first approached the powerhouse and then all fish that first approached the spillway. Differences between fish species and years will be presented within these sections.

A basic understanding of how we arranged the data in the tables will help interpret the results. Table 6 is an example of the how the results for the one-step analysis are presented. Particular attention should be given to the table caption to determine the year (2006, 2007, 2008, or 2009) and approach criteria (regardless of approach, first approach in the powerhouse, and first approach in the spillway) that is represented in the table. The "Area of Passage" in the first row of the table represents the states upstream of the dam starting in the south powerhouse area (PH#1) and continuing north to the end of the spillway (SP#3). Within each area, the probability of passing the dam is shown for each species. In the following example, the probability of yearling Chinook salmon passing into the juvenile bypass system (JBS) from PH#1 is 0.17, and the probability of passing through the turbines is 0.04. Within each area, the probabilities are cumulative, so for this example, the probability of passing either the JBS or turbines in PH#1 is 0.21. Another way to interpret this result is that 0.21 of the fish that entered into PH#1 passed the dam (either through the JBS or turbines) and the remaining 0.79 transitioned to an adjoining area (for example, PH#2). It is important to understand that the probabilities are not cumulative across adjoining areas. The superscript letters associated with each of the probabilities in the table represent the robustness of the estimate, with the letter "a" being the most robust (greater than 100 transitions were used to estimate the probability) and the letter "c" being the least (10–50 transitions were used to estimate the probabilities). Probabilities based on less than 10 transitions are represented by an asterisk (*) and were not presented in the tables. A back slash (\) is used to show that a passage alternative (for example, TSW) was not installed and therefore unavailable for fish to use during that year.

The presentation of results for the two-step analysis is very similar to that of the one-step analysis. The main difference is where the fish was located before it moved to the next area. In the following example (table 7), 0.34 of the steelhead passed through the spillway in the SP#1 area after first moving to SP#1 from PH#3; whereas, 0.21 of the steelhead moved through the SP#1 area after first traveling from SP#2 to SP#1. When interpreting the results from the two-step analysis, it is important to note where the fish first approached the dam. For example, for fish that first approached the powerhouse, there are no data for fish that passed any of the spillway areas (SP#1, SP#2, or SP#3) after transitioning from the forebay because only the fish that were first detected in the powerhouse are included in the table. The same is true for fish that first approached the spillway. There are no data for fish that passed any of the powerhouse areas after transitioning from the forebay because only the fish that first approached the spillway are included in the table. For completeness, the tables include all columns for fish approaching from the forebay but table cells have an "NA" (not applicable) for passage areas different than approach area. The two-step analysis allowed us to investigate how the transitions from one state depended on which state the fish was in previously.

One-Step Markov Chain

Transition Probabilities Regardless of Area of First Detection

In 2006, the highest proportions of fish transitioning through a passage route occurred in the spillway (table 6). Within the spillway, 0.80 of the yearling Chinook salmon that entered the SP#1 area passed through the bays in the SP#1 area and the remaining 0.20 transitioned to adjoining areas. After entering one of the three areas in the spillway, the probability of steelhead passing the spillway was highest for fish in the SP#3 area (0.47), less for fish in the SP#1 area (0.31), and lowest for fish in the SP#2 area (0.20). For all species, the probability of passing the spillway was lowest after entering the SP#2 area. Subyearling Chinook salmon exhibited a relatively high probability of passage after entering the SP#3 area (0.81).

Within the powerhouse area, transitions into passage routes were lowest for steelhead compared to the other two species. Only 0.02 to 0.11 of steelhead that entered into one of the three areas in the powerhouse passed into either the JBS or turbines. The remaining 0.89 to 0.98 of steelhead transitioned to adjoining areas before passing the dam. Compared to steelhead, more yearling Chinook salmon (0.04–0.17) that entered one of the three areas in the powerhouse passed the powerhouse through either the JBS or turbines, and about the same proportion of subyearling Chinook salmon (0.05–0.11) passed the powerhouse. Regardless of species, more fish consistently passed through the JBS compared to the turbines after entering one of the three areas upstream of the powerhouse.

The operation of the TSWs in bays 22 and 20 during 2007 produced an increase in passage probabilities in the spillway (table 8). After entering the SP#1 area, the proportion of fish passing through all routes in the SP#1 area remained nearly the same for yearling Chinook salmon in 2007 (0.82) and 2006 (0.80), however, their route of passage within the SP#1 area changed substantially. After entering the SP#1 area, the proportion that passed though the bays in this area decreased from 0.80 in 2006 to 0.26 in 2007, but the proportion passing through both TSWs was 0.56. For steelhead, the proportion of fish passing through all routes in the SP#1 area increased from 0.31 in 2006 to 0.70 in 2007. A similar trend was apparent for subyearling Chinook salmon with an increase from 0.39 in 2006 to 0.78 in 2007. Of the two TSWs, the one in bay 22 accounted for a higher proportion of fish passing in the SP#1 area, thereby decreasing the proportion of fish that transition to other areas of the dam before passing.

Table 6. Percentage of fish passing McNary Dam during day and night periods in 2006 based on a one-step Markov Chain analysis.

[Data represent all fish regardless of where they first approached the dam and include both day and night periods. Species: YCH, Yearling Chinook salmon; STH, juvenile steelhead; SCH, subyearling Chinook salmon. Area of Passage: PH#1, turbine units 1–5; PH#2, turbine units 6–10; PH#3, turbine units 11–14; SP#1, spill bays 16–22; SP#2, spill bays 7–15; SP#3, spill bays 1–6; JBS, juvenile bypass system; TSW, temporary spillway weir. The (/) denotes the TSW was not installed at this time. Superscripts denote number of transitions used to calculate percentage: [a], greater than 100; [b], 50 to 100]

| | Area of Passage | | | | | | | | | | | |
| Species | PH #1 | | PH #2 | | PH #3 | | SP #1 | | | SP #2 | SP #3 | |
	JBS	Turbine	JBS	Turbine	JBS	Turbine	TSW 22	TSW 20	Bays	Bays	Bays	TSW 4
YCH	17[a]	4[a]	17[a]	7[a]	17[a]	11[a]	/	/	80[a]	49[a]	59[a]	/
STH	11[a]	3[a]	5[a]	2[a]	5[a]	2[a]	/	/	31[a]	20[a]	47[a]	/
SCH	11[a]	10[a]	7[a]	10[a]	5[a]	9[a]	/	/	39[a]	36[a]	81[b]	/

Table 7. Percentage of fish passing McNary Dam during day and night periods in 2006 based on a two-step Markov Chain analysis.

[Data represent all fish regardless of where they first approached the dam and include both day and night periods. Species: YCH, Yearling Chinook salmon; STH, juvenile steelhead; SCH, subyearling Chinook salmon. Area of Passage: Service Bay, equipment service bay on the southern end of powerhouse; PH#1, turbine units 1–5; PH#2, turbine units 6–10; PH#3, turbine units 11–14; SP#1, spill bays 16–22; SP#2, spill bays 7–15; SP#3, spill bays 1–6; JBS, juvenile bypass system; Turb, turbine units; TSW, temporary spillway weir; Bays, area spill bays. The (\) denotes the TSW was not installed at this time. Superscripts denote number of transitions used to calculate percentage, a > 100; b = 50 to 100; c = 10 to 50; (*) = < 10, which was insufficient sample size to calculate percentage]

Area of Passage:	PH #1						PH #2					
	passing PH#1 after coming from Service Bay		passing PH#1 after coming from forebay		passing PH#1 after coming from PH#2		passing PH#2 after coming from PH#1		passing PH#2 after coming from forebay		passing PH#2 after coming from PH#3	
Species	JBS	Turb	JBS	Turb	JBS	Turb	JBS	Turb	JBS	Turb	JBS	Turb
YCH	18^a	6^a	32^a	7^a	9^a	2^a	11^a	5^a	34^a	14^a	13^a	4^a
STH	9^b	3^b	22^a	4^a	7^a	2^a	4^a	1^a	15^a	5^a	3^a	1^a
SCH	11^a	12^a	18^a	15^a	8^a	8^a	5^a	11^a	12^a	14^a	7^a	7^a

Area of Passage:	PH #3						SP #1								
	passing PH#3 after coming from PH#2		passing PH#3 after coming from forebay		passing PH#3 after coming from SP#1		passing SP#1 after coming from PH#3			passing SP#1 after coming from forebay			passing SP#1 after coming from SP#2		
Species	JBS	Turb	JBS	Turb	JBS	Turb	TSW 22	TSW 20	Bays	TSW 22	TSW 20	Bays	TSW 22	TSW 20	Bays
YCH	13^a	8^a	26^a	18^a	0^c	6^c	\	\	85^a	\	\	68^b	\	\	81^b
STH	3^a	1^a	11^a	11^a	7^a	1^a	\	\	34^a	\	\	36^b	\	\	21^a
SCH	4^a	7^a	8^a	15^a	2^b	4^b	\	\	48^a	\	\	11^c	\	\	22^c

Area of Passage:	SP #2			SP #3			
	passing SP#2 after coming from SP#1	passing SP#2 after coming from forebay	passing SP#2 after coming from SP#3	passing SP1#3 after coming from SP#2		passing SP#3 after coming from forebay	
Species	Bays	Bays	Bays	Bays	TSW 4	Bays	TSW 4
YCH	51^c	54^a	36^b	65^b	\	54^b	\
STH	20^a	38^b	7^b	50^a	\	36^c	\
SCH	42^a	22^c	9^c	90^b	\	*	\

After entering one of the three areas upstream of the powerhouse, the probability of passing the powerhouse in 2007 was similar to 2006 for all species (table 8). Once again, the probability of steelhead passing the powerhouse through either the JBS or turbines was lower compared to the other species. Similar to 2006, all species had a higher probability of passing the JBS compared to the turbines across all three areas of the powerhouse during 2007.

The relocation of the TSW during 2008 from bay 22 to bay 19 affected passage probabilities in the SP#1 area. After fish entered the SP#1 area, overall passage proportions through this area decreased by about 0.08 to 0.10 and the proportions passing through both TSWs combined decreased in 2008 compared to 2007 (table 9). The combined passage probabilities for the two TSWs decreased from 0.56 to 0.45 for yearling Chinook salmon, 0.61 to 0.44 for steelhead, and 0.60 to 0.36 for subyearling Chinook salmon. Of the yearling Chinook salmon that entered the SP#1 area, the proportion that passed through the bays remained about the same in 2007 and 2008. For steelhead and subyearling Chinook salmon, the number of fish passing the bays in the SP#1 area increased from 2007 to 2008. Trends in passage probabilities in the powerhouse remained constant in 2008 compared to the two previous years.

In 2009, changes in the locations of the TSW resulted in changes in the passage proportions among the three areas of the spillway. During the spring study period, one TSW was located in bay 20 (within the SP#1 area) and one was located in bay 4 (within the SP#3 area). With only one TSW within the SP#1 area, the total passage probability through the remaining TSW and bays combined decreased for yearling Chinook salmon from 0.69 in 2008 to 0.59 in 2009 (table 10). Similarly, of the fish that entered the SP#1 area, passage probabilities in the SP#1 area in 2009 for steelhead decreased from 0.59 in 2008 to 0.43 in 2009. During the summer study period, the TSW located in bay 4 was moved back to bay 19 resulting in two TSW within the SP#1 area, similar to 2007 and 2008. Of the fish that entered the SP#1 area, passage probabilities through all routes in the SP#1 area remained relatively high for subyearling Chinook salmon in 2009 (0.68), which was similar to 2008 (0.70) and 0.10 lower than 2007 (0.78).

The presence of the TSW in the SP#3 area during spring 2009 appeared to have a positive effect on passage probabilities (table 10). During 2009, passage probabilities through all routes in the SP#3 area for yearling Chinook salmon that entered this area was 0.68, which was an increase from what was observed in 2006 (0.59), 2007 (0.27), and 2008 (0.21) when no TSW was located in the SP#3 area. For steelhead that entered the SP#3 area, passage probabilities were highest in 2009 when the TSW was in the SP#3 area (0.49). This was similar to what was observed in 2006 (0.47) and higher than the proportion that passed this area in 2007 (0.14) and 2008 (0.17). During the 3 years the TSWs were tested, similar trends were observed in the SP#3 area for subyearling Chinook salmon. Of the fish that entered the SP#3 area, passage probabilities were highest in 2009 (0.55) when the TSW was present and lower in 2007 (0.40) and 2008 (0.35) when no TSW was in this area.

Regardless of where fish first approached the dam, there were differences in passage probabilities during the day and night, especially after fish entered one of the three areas upstream of the powerhouse. The trends varied among the three species and across the 4 years included in the analysis. The passage trends in the spillway remained about the same during the day and night. The results of the one-step analysis for all fish regardless of where they first approached the dam during the day and night are presented in appendix B. The effect of diel period on the passage probabilities is discussed in more detail in the section describing transition probabilities during day and night for fish that first approached the powerhouse and first approached the spillway.

Table 8. Percentage of fish passing McNary Dam during day and night periods in 2007 based on a one-step Markov Chain analysis.

[Data represent all fish regardless of where they first approached the dam and include both day and night periods. Species: YCH, Yearling Chinook salmon; STH, juvenile steelhead; SCH, subyearling Chinook salmon. Area of Passage: PH#1, turbine units 1–5; PH#2, turbine units 6–10; PH#3, turbine units 11–14; SP#1, spill bays 16–22; SP#2, spill bays 7–15; SP#3, spill bays 1–6; JBS, juvenile bypass system; Turb, turbine units; TSW, temporary spillway weir; Bays, area spill bays. The (\) denotes the TSW was not installed at this time. Superscripts denote number of transitions used to calculate percentage, a > 100; b = 50 to 100; c = 10 to 50; (*) = < 10, which was insufficient sample size to calculate percentage]

| | PH #1 | | PH #2 | | PH #3 | | SP #1 | | | SP #2 | SP #3 | |
| | | | | | | | Area of Passage | | | | | |
Species	JBS	Turbine	JBS	Turbine	JBS	Turbine	TSW 22	TSW 20	Bays	Bays	Bays	TSW 4
YCH	18[a]	4[a]	24[a]	3[a]	10[a]	8[a]	41[a]	15[a]	26[a]	34[a]	27[b]	\
STH	4[a]	2[a]	4[a]	0[a]	3[a]	1[a]	45[a]	16[a]	9[a]	6[a]	14[a]	\
SCH	17[a]	5[a]	17[a]	4[a]	5[a]	9[a]	41[a]	19[a]	18[a]	18[b]	40[c]	\

Table 9. Percentage of fish passing McNary Dam during day and night periods in 2008 based on a one-step Markov Chain analysis.

[Data represent all fish regardless of where they first approached the dam and include both day and night periods. Species: YCH, Yearling Chinook salmon; STH, juvenile steelhead; SCH, subyearling Chinook salmon. Area of Passage: PH#1, turbine units 1–5; PH#2, turbine units 6–10; PH#3, turbine units 11–14; SP#1, spill bays 16–22; SP#2, spill bays 7–15; SP#3, spill bays 1–6; JBS, juvenile bypass system; Turb, turbine units; TSW, temporary spillway weir; Bays, area spill bays. The (\) denotes the TSW was not installed at this time. Superscripts denote number of transitions used to calculate percentage, a > 100; b = 50 to 100; c = 10 to 50; (*) = < 10, which was insufficient sample size to calculate percentage]

| | PH #1 | | PH #2 | | PH #3 | | SP #1 | | | SP #2 | SP #3 | |
| | | | | | | | Area of Passage | | | | | |
Species	JBS	Turbine	JBS	Turbine	JBS	Turbine	TSW 20	TSW 19	Bays	Bays	Bays	TSW 4
YCH	15[a]	5[a]	14[a]	7[a]	10[a]	13[a]	22[a]	23[a]	24[a]	9[c]	21[c]	\
STH	10[a]	2[a]	5[a]	2[a]	4[a]	6[a]	28[a]	16[a]	15[a]	8[a]	17[b]	\
SCH	11[a]	11[a]	6[a]	10[a]	2[a]	14[a]	19[a]	17[a]	34[a]	16[b]	35[c]	\

Table 10. Percentage of fish passing McNary Dam during day and night periods in 2009 based on a one-step Markov Chain analysis.

[Data represent all fish regardless of where they first approached the dam and include both day and night periods. Species: YCH, Yearling Chinook salmon; STH, juvenile steelhead; SCH, subyearling Chinook salmon. Area of Passage: PH#1, turbine units 1–5; PH#2, turbine units 6–10; PH#3, turbine units 11–14; SP#1, spill bays 16–22; SP#2, spill bays 7–15; SP#3, spill bays 1–6; JBS, juvenile bypass system; Turb, turbine units; TSW, temporary spillway weir; Bays, area spill bays. The (\) denotes the TSW was not installed at this time. Superscripts denote number of transitions used to calculate percentage, a > 100; b = 50 to 100; c = 10 to 50; (*) = < 10, which was insufficient sample size to calculate percentage]

Area of Passage

Species	PH #1		PH #2		PH #3			SP #1		SP #2	SP #3	
	JBS	Turbine	JBS	Turbine	JBS	Turbine	TSW 20	TSW 19	Bays	Bays	Bays	TSW 4
YCH	15[a]	5[a]	12[a]	5[a]	19[a]	9[a]	21[a]	\	38[a]	52[a]	40[a]	28[a]
STH	9[a]	2[a]	7[a]	1[a]	8[a]	1[a]	28[a]	\	15[a]	21[a]	20[a]	29[a]
SCH	9[a]	7[a]	4[a]	7[a]	14[a]	15[a]	25[a]	21[a]	22[a]	48[a]	55[a]	\

Transition Probabilities after First Approaching the Powerhouse

The area in which a fish first approached the dam influenced passage probabilities. During 2006, fish that first approached the powerhouse and subsequently entered one of the three areas upstream of the powerhouse had passage probabilities between 0.06 and 0.29 through the JBS and turbines combined, with the remaining 0.71 to 0.94 of the fish transitioning to adjoining areas (table 11). Between 0.32 and 0.86 of the fish that transitioned to SP#1 after approaching the powerhouse passed through the bays in the SP#1 area. Passage probabilities were lower for each species in the SP#2 area than in the SP#1 area but higher for steelhead and subyearling Chinook salmon in the SP#3 area.

The installation of the TSWs in 2007 increased passage probabilities in the SP#1 area. After fish entered the SP#1 area, passage through all routes in this area increased by 0.06 for yearling Chinook salmon, 0.43 for steelhead, and 0.33 for subyearling Chinook salmon (table 12). Of the yearling Chinook salmon that were first detected in the powerhouse area, the majority of them transitioned into the spillway. After entering the SP#1 area, a larger proportion (0.92) passed the dam and the remaining 0.08 transitioned to an adjoining area. The majority of the yearling Chinook salmon that passed the dam after entering the SP#1 area passed through the TSW in bay 22 (0.75) and relatively few (0.07) passed through the TSW in bay 20 or the other bays in the SP#1 area (0.10). Passage of steelhead increased from 0.32 in 2006 to 0.75 in 2007 with the majority (0.60) passing through the TSW in bay 22. A similar pattern was observed for subyearling Chinook salmon. Total passage through all routes in the SP#1 area after fish entered that area increased from 0.47 in 2006 to 0.80 in 2007 with the majority (0.54) of fish passing through the TSW in bay 22 and a smaller proportion passing through TSW 20 (0.13).

Moving the TSW in 2008 from bay 22 to bay 19 had an effect on passage probabilities in the SP#1 area for fish that were first detected in the powerhouse. Having both TSWs in the SP#1 area during 2008 resulted in increased passage probabilities for steelhead and subyearling Chinook salmon compared to 2006, but it was not as high as the probabilities observed in 2007 (table 13). Of the fish that first approached the dam in the powerhouse area and moved into the SP#1 area, the proportion of steelhead that passed the dam remained high in 2008 (0.67). This was an increase compared to 2006 (0.32), but a decrease from what was observed in 2007 (0.75). The pattern was similar for subyearling Chinook salmon. Of the subyearling Chinook salmon that entered the SP#1 area, passage probabilities through all routes combined in the SP#1 area were high in 2008 (0.72) compared to 2006 (0.47), but were about the same compared to 2007 (0.80). Passage probabilities in the SP#1 area were relatively high for yearling Chinook salmon in 2006 (0.86) and increased in 2007 (0.92), but decreased in 2008 (0.75).

The decrease in passage in the SP#1 area that was observed in 2008 continued in 2009, likely a result of having only one TSW in this area during the spring study period. As was the case in previous years, after first being detected in the powerhouse areas, greater than 0.70 of all species transitioned out of the powerhouse areas into adjoining areas (table 14). After fish entered the SP#1 area, passage probabilities in the SP#1 area were high in 2009 compared to 2006, but lower for some species than what was observed during the other 2 years (2007 and 2008) when TSWs were tested (table 15). The addition of the TSW to the SP#3 area during the spring study season in 2009 increased passage probabilities in that area for fish that were first detected in the powerhouse.

Table 11. Percentage of fish passing McNary Dam during day and night periods in 2006 based on a one-step Markov Chain analysis.

[Data represent all fish that first approached the powerhouse and include both day and night periods. Species: YCH, Yearling Chinook salmon; STH, juvenile steelhead; SCH, subyearling Chinook salmon. Area of Passage: PH#1, turbine units 1–5; PH#2, turbine units 6–10; PH#3, turbine units 11–14; SP#1, spill bays 16–22; SP#2, spill bays 7–15; SP#3, spill bays 1–6; JBS, juvenile bypass system; Turb, turbine units; TSW, temporary spillway weir; Bays, area spill bays. The (\) denotes the TSW was not installed at this time. Superscripts denote number of transitions used to calculate percentage, a > 100; b = 50 to 100; c = 10 to 50; (*) = <10, which was insufficient sample size to calculate percentage]

| | PH #1 | | PH #2 | | PH #3 | | SP #1 | | | SP #2 | SP #3 | |
| | | | | | | | Area of Passage | | | | | |
Species	JBS	Turbine	JBS	Turbine	JBS	Turbine	TSW 22	TSW 20	Bays	Bays	Bays	TSW 4
YCH	17a	4a	17a	7a	17a	12a	\	\	86a	14c	*	\
STH	10a	3a	5a	2a	4a	2a	\	\	32a	17a	46b	\
SCH	11a	10a	7a	11a	5a	10a	\	\	47a	43b	94c	\

Table 12. Percentage of fish passing McNary Dam during day and night periods in 2007 based on a one-step Markov Chain analysis.

[Data represent all fish that first approached the powerhouse and include both day and night periods. Species: YCH, Yearling Chinook salmon; STH, juvenile steelhead; SCH, subyearling Chinook salmon. Area of Passage: PH#1, turbine units 1–5; PH#2, turbine units 6–10; PH#3, turbine units 11–14; SP#1, spill bays 16–22; SP#2, spill bays 7–15; SP#3, spill bays 1–6; JBS, juvenile bypass system; Turb, turbine units; TSW, temporary spillway weir; Bays, area spill bays. The (\) denotes the TSW was not installed at this time. Superscripts denote number of transitions used to calculate percentage, a > 100; b = 50 to 100; c = 10 to 50; (*) = <10, which was insufficient sample size to calculate percentage]

| | PH #1 | | PH #2 | | PH #3 | | SP #1 | | | SP #2 | SP #3 | |
| | | | | | | | Area of Passage | | | | | |
Species	JBS	Turbine	JBS	Turbine	JBS	Turbine	TSW 22	TSW 20	Bays	Bays	Bays	TSW 4
YCH	18a	4a	24a	3a	11a	8a	75a	7a	10a	27c	*	\
STH	4a	2a	4a	0a	3a	1a	60a	11a	4a	2a	25c	\
SCH	17a	5a	17a	5a	5a	9a	54a	13a	13a	28c	*	\

Table 13. Percentage of fish passing McNary Dam during day and night periods in 2008 based on a one-step Markov Chain analysis.

[Data represent all fish that first approached the powerhouse and include both day and night periods. Species: YCH, Yearling Chinook salmon; STH, juvenile steelhead; SCH, subyearling Chinook salmon. Area of Passage: PH#1, turbine units 1–5; PH#2, turbine units 6–10; PH#3, turbine units 11–14; SP#1, spill bays 16–22; SP#2, spill bays 7–15; SP#3, spill bays 1–6; JBS, juvenile bypass system; Turb, turbine units; TSW, temporary spillway weir; Bays, area spill bays. The (\) denotes the TSW was not installed at this time. Superscripts denote number of transitions used to calculate percentage, a > 100; b = 50 to 100; c = 10 to 50; (*) = < 10, which was insufficient sample size to calculate percentage]

	PH #1		PH #2		PH #3		SP #1			SP #2	SP #3	
Species	JBS	Turbine	JBS	Turbine	JBS	Turbine	TSW 20	TSW 19	Bays	Bays	Bays	TSW 4
YCH	15[a]	5[a]	14[a]	8[a]	10[a]	10[a]	32[a]	14[a]	29[a]	11[c]	*	\
STH	11[a]	3[a]	7[a]	2[a]	4[a]	6[a]	37[a]	14[a]	16[a]	11[c]	44[c]	\
SCH	12[a]	11[a]	6[a]	10[a]	2[a]	13[a]	19[a]	15[a]	38[a]	29[c]	64[c]	\

Table 14. Percentage of fish passing McNary Dam during day and night periods in 2009 based on a one-step Markov Chain analysis.

[Data represent all fish that first approached the powerhouse and include both day and night periods. Species: YCH, Yearling Chinook salmon; STH, juvenile steelhead; SCH, subyearling Chinook salmon. Area of Passage: PH#1, turbine units 1–5; PH#2, turbine units 6–10; PH#3, turbine units 11–14; SP#1, spill bays 16–22; SP#2, spill bays 7–15; SP#3, spill bays 1–6; JBS, juvenile bypass system; Turb, turbine units; TSW, temporary spillway weir; Bays, area spill bays. The (\) denotes the TSW was not installed at this time. Superscripts denote number of transitions used to calculate percentage, a > 100; b = 50 to 100; c = 10 to 50; (*) = < 10, which was insufficient sample size to calculate percentage]

	PH #1		PH #2		PH #3		SP #1			SP #2	SP #3	
Species	JBS	Turbine	JBS	Turbine	JBS	Turbine	TSW 20	TSW 19	Bays	Bays	Bays	TSW 4
YCH	15[a]	5[a]	12[a]	5[a]	19[a]	8[a]	22[a]	\	49[a]	46[c]	42[c]	50[c]
STH	9[a]	1[a]	7[a]	2[a]	6[a]	1[a]	30[a]	\	16[a]	15[a]	17[a]	30[a]
SCH	9[a]	7[a]	4[a]	7[a]	15[a]	15[a]	32[a]	8[a]	30[a]	37[b]	61[c]	0[c]

Table 15. Percentage of fish passing McNary Dam through all routes combined (TSW and standard bays) within the SP#1 area by species and study year during day and night periods from 2006 to 2009 based on a one-step Markov Chain analysis.

[Data represent all fish that first approached the powerhouse and include both day and night periods. Area of Passage: SP#1, spill bays 16–22. Superscripts denote number of transitions used to calculate percentage, a > 100; b = 50 to 100; c = 10 to 50; (*) = <10, which was insufficient sample size to calculate percentage. TSWs were not installed during 2006 and only one of the two TSW was installed in the SP#1 area during the spring of 2009 when yearling Chinook salmon and steelhead pass]

Passage through the SP#1 area by study year

Species	2006	2007	2008	2009
Yearling Chinook Salmon	86[a]	92[a]	75[a]	71[a]
Steelhead	32[a]	75[a]	67[a]	46[a]
Subyearling Chinook Salmon	47[a]	80[a]	72[a]	70[a]

33

Transition Probabilities after First Approaching the Spillway

During 2006, 0.74 or less of the fish that first approached one of the three areas in the spillway passed the dam in that area with the remaining fish transitioning to an adjoining area before passing (table 16). Most fish transitioned to one of the other two areas in the spillway (SP#2 and SP#3) and passed the dam. Compared to fish that were first detected in the powerhouse in 2006, we observed higher passage probabilities in the three powerhouse areas for all species that were first detected in the spillway. This indicated that a higher proportion of fish that were first detected in the spillway transitioned to the powerhouse before passing the dam compared to the proportion of fish that passed the dam through the powerhouse after first being detected in the powerhouse. This trend also was observed in 2007 for yearling Chinook salmon, even with the addition of the TSW to the SP#1 area (table 17). After fish entered the SP#1 area, passage of yearling Chinook salmon through this area remained about the same in 2007 (0.77) compared to 2006 (0.74). This was not the case for the other two species. Passage probabilities for fish first detected in the spillway increased substantially in the SP#1 area, increasing from 0.27 in 2006 to 0.63 in 2007 for steelhead and increasing from 0.22 to 0.75 for subyearling Chinook salmon.

Moving the TSWs during 2008 impacted passage probabilities for fish that were first detected in the spillway. Of the fish that entered the SP#1 area, passage probabilities for all routes in that area decreased from 0.77 in 2007 to 0.63 in 2008 for yearling Chinook salmon (table 18). The proportion of steelhead that passed through the SP#1 area decreases from 0.63 in 2007 to 0.47 in 2008 and much of the decrease was attributed to the relatively low passage probabilities through TSW 20 in 2008 (0.14) compared to TSW 22 in 2007 (0.24). Passage probabilities through all routes in the SP#1 area decreased from 0.75 in 2007 to 0.68 in 2008 for subyearling Chinook salmon with much of the decrease attributed to passage through the TSWs.

Passage probabilities in the SP#1 area during 2009 for fish that were first detected in the spillway were affected by having only one TSW as a passage alternative in this area. The overall passage through the SP#1 area decreased to 0.52 and 0.40 for both yearling Chinook salmon and steelhead (table 19). Instead of passing through the SP#1 area, fish tended to transition to the SP#2 and SP#3 areas and pass through the standard bays. The addition of the TWS to the SP#3 area did result in more fish passing that area. Across all years, the configuration that resulted in more fish passing the SP#1 area after first being detected the spillway was during 2007 (table 20).

Table 16. Percentage of fish passing McNary Dam during day and night periods in 2006 based on a one-step Markov Chain analysis.

[Data represent all fish that first approached the spillway and include both day and night periods. Species: YCH, Yearling Chinook salmon; STH, juvenile steelhead; SCH, subyearling Chinook salmon. Area of Passage: PH#1, turbine units 1–5; PH#2, turbine units 6–10; PH#3, turbine units 11–14; SP#1, spill bays 16–22; SP#2, spill bays 7–15; SP#3, spill bays 1–6; JBS, juvenile bypass system;Turb, turbine units; TSW, temporary spillway weir; Bays, area spill bays. The (\) denotes the TSW was not installed at this time. Superscripts denote number of transitions used to calculate percentage, a > 100; b = 50 to 100; c = 10 to 50; (*) = < 10, which was insufficient sample size to calculate percentage]

Area of Passage

| | PH #1 | | PH #2 | | PH #3 | | SP #1 | | | SP #2 | SP #3 | |
	JBS	Turbine	JBS	Turbine	JBS	Turbine	TSW 22	TSW 20	Bays	Bays	Bays	TSW 4
YCH	*	*	21c	5c	9c	0c	\	\	74a	52a	58a	\
STH	12b	5b	4a	2a	6a	1a	\	\	27a	24a	49b	\
SCH	7b	13b	0b	6b	1b	1b			22b	27b	61c	\

Table 17. Percentage of fish passing McNary Dam during day and night periods in 2007 based on a one-step Markov Chain analysis.

[Data represent all fish that first approached the spillway and include both day and night periods. Species: YCH, Yearling Chinook salmon; STH, juvenile steelhead; SCH, subyearling Chinook salmon. Area of Passage: PH#1, turbine units 1–5; PH#2, turbine units 6–10; PH#3, turbine units 11–14; SP#1, spill bays 16–22; SP#2, spill bays 7–15; SP#3, spill bays 1–6; JBS, juvenile bypass system; Turb, turbine units; TSW, temporary spillway weir; Bays, area spill bays. The (\) denotes the TSW was not installed at this time. Superscripts denote number of transitions used to calculate percentage, a > 100; b = 50 to 100; c = 10 to 50; (*) = < 10, which was insufficient sample size to calculate percentage]

Area of Passage

| | PH #1 | | PH #2 | | PH #3 | | SP #1 | | | SP #2 | SP #3 | |
Species	JBS	Turbine	JBS	Turbine	JBS	Turbine	TSW 22	TSW 20	Bays	Bays	Bays	TSW 4
YCH	16c	0c	29c	6c	5b	17b	19a	20a	38a	35a	24b	\
STH	4a	2a	5a	0a	3a	1a	24a	23a	16a	7a	8b	\
SCH	21c	0c	9c	2c	7c	9c	25a	26a	24a	15b	26c	\

Table 18. Percentage of fish passing McNary Dam during day and night periods in 2008 based on a one-step Markov Chain analysis.

[Data represent all fish that first approached the spillway and include both day and night periods. Species: YCH, Yearling Chinook salmon; STH, juvenile steelhead; SCH, subyearling Chinook salmon. Area of Passage: PH#1, turbine units 1–5; PH#2, turbine units 6–10; PH#3, turbine units 11–14; SP#1, spill bays 16–22; SP#2, spill bays 7–15; SP#3, spill bays 1–6; JBS, juvenile bypass system; Turb, turbine units; TSW, temporary spillway weir; Bays, area spill bays. The (\) denotes the TSW was not installed at this time. Superscripts denote number of transitions used to calculate percentage, a > 100; b = 50 to 100; c = 10 to 50; (*) = < 10, which was insufficient sample size to calculate percentage]

| | Area of Passage | | | | | | | | | | | |
| | PH #1 | | PH #2 | | PH #3 | | SP #1 | | | SP #2 | SP #3 | |
Species	JBS	Turbine	JBS	Turbine	JBS	Turbine	TSW 20	TSW 19	Bays	Bays	Bays	TSW 4
YCH	12[c]	0[c]	11[c]	3[c]	8[b]	28[b]	14[a]	29[a]	20[a]	8[b]	22[c]	\
STH	8[c]	0[c]	0[b]	1[b]	3[a]	6[a]	14[a]	18[a]	15[a]	7[a]	5[c]	\
SCH	0[c]	3[c]	0[c]	3[c]	2[c]	21[c]	18[a]	20[a]	30[a]	7[c]	8[c]	\

Table 19. Percentage of fish passing McNary Dam during day and night periods in 2009 based on a one-step Markov Chain analysis.

[Data represent all fish that first approached the spillway and include both day and night periods. Species: YCH, Yearling Chinook salmon; STH, juvenile steelhead; SCH, subyearling Chinook salmon. Area of Passage: PH#1, turbine units 1–5; PH#2, turbine units 6–10; PH#3, turbine units 11–14; SP#1, spill bays 16–22; SP#2, spill bays 7–15; SP#3, spill bays 1–6; JBS, juvenile bypass system; Turb, turbine units TSW, temporary spillway weir; Bays, area spill bays. The (\) denotes the TSW was not installed at this time. Superscripts denote number of transitions used to calculate percentage, a > 100; b = 50 to 100; c = 10 to 50; (*) = < 10, which was insufficient sample size to calculate percentage]

| | Area of Passage | | | | | | | | | | | |
| | PH #1 | | PH #2 | | PH #3 | | SP #1 | | | SP #2 | SP #3 | |
Species	JBS	Turbine	JBS	Turbine	JBS	Turbine	TSW 20	TSW 19	Bays	Bays	Bays	TSW 4
YCH	16[c]	16[c]	19[c]	8[c]	21[b]	15[b]	21[a]	\	31[a]	53[a]	40[a]	26[a]
STH	6[a]	2[a]	7[a]	0[a]	14[a]	1[a]	26[a]	\	14[a]	25[a]	21[a]	28[a]
SCH	0[c]	4[c]	0[c]	11[c]	13[b]	18[b]	17[a]	33[a]	14[a]	51[a]	54[a]	\

Table 20. Percentage of fish passing McNary Dam through all routes combined (TSW and standard bays) within the SP#1 area by species and study year during day and night periods from 2006 to 2009 based on a one-step Markov Chain analysis.

[Data represent all fish that first approached the spillway and include both day and night periods. Area of Passage: SP#1, spill bays 16–22. Superscripts denote number of transitions used to calculate percentage, a > 100; b = 50 to 100; c = 10 to 50; (*) = < 10, which was insufficient sample size to calculate percentage. TSWs were not installed during 2006 and only one of the two TSW was installed in the SP#1 area during the spring of 2009 when yearling Chinook salmon and steelhead pass]

	Passage through the SP#1 area by study year			
Species	2006	2007	2008	2009
Yearling Chinook Salmon	74[a]	77[a]	63[a]	52[a]
Steelhead	27[a]	63[a]	47[a]	40[a]
Subyearling Chinook Salmon	22[b]	75[a]	68[a]	64[a]

Transition Probabilities during Day and Night for Fish that First Approached the Powerhouse

Passage probabilities during day and night periods varied among species and across study years. The results for fish that first approached the powerhouse during the day and during the night are presented first, followed by the results for fish that first approached the spillway. In 2006, daytime passage was higher than nighttime passage in the SP#1 area for fish that first approached the powerhouse (tables 21 and 22). In general, the opposite was observed in the powerhouse areas where passage proportions were higher during the night than the day, particularly for steelhead.

During 2007, a greater proportion of steelhead and subyearling Chinook salmon passed through the SP#1 area during the day compared to the night, primarily through the two TSWs in bays 20 and 22 (tables 23 and 24). The passage probability for steelhead through all passage routes in the SP#1 area was 0.82 during the day and 0.60 during the night. Similarly, the passage probability for subyearling Chinook salmon was 0.86 during the day and 0.73 during the night. The passage probability for yearling Chinook salmon remained about the same during the day (0.91) and night (0.94). If only fish that passed through the two TSWs are considered, the passage trends were similar for all three species. Passage through the two TSWs was consistently higher during the day, compared to the night, for all three species. The probability of passing the powerhouse during the day or night was variable among the species, but was generally higher during the day for subyearling Chinook salmon, lower during the day for steelhead, and about the same between day and night for yearling Chinook salmon.

After fish entered the SP#1 area, passage probabilities for all routes combined in this area were consistently higher during the day compared to the night for all three species in 2008 (tables 25 and 26). Passage probabilities during the day for all routes combined in the SP#1 area increased by 0.24 for yearling Chinook salmon (0.85 day, 0.61 night), by 0.25 for steelhead (0.78 day, 0.53 night), and by 0.20 for subyearling Chinook salmon (0.78 day, 0.58 night). If only the fish that passed through the two TSWs combined are considered, daytime passage remained higher than nighttime passage for steelhead, remained about the same for yearling Chinook salmon, and was slightly higher during the night, compared to day, for subyearling Chinook salmon. Passage through the powerhouse routes remained about the same during the day and night for yearling Chinook salmon and subyearling Chinook salmon but passage was noticeably higher during the night for steelhead. Similar patterns in passage probabilities were observed during 2009. Passage probabilities within the SP#1 area remained higher during the day compared to night for yearling Chinook salmon and steelhead and were about the same during day and night for subyearling Chinook salmon (tables 27 and 28).

Table 21. Percentage of fish passing McNary Dam during day period in 2006 based on a one-step Markov Chain analysis.

[Data represent all fish that first approached the powerhouse during the day period. Species: YCH, Yearling Chinook salmon; STH, juvenile steelhead; SCH, subyearling Chinook salmon. Area of Passage: PH#1, turbine units 1–5; PH#2, turbine units 6–10; PH#3, turbine units 11–14; SP#1, spill bays 16–22; SP#2, spill bays 1–6; SP#3, spill bays 7–15; SP#2, spill bays 1–6; JBS, juvenile bypass system; Turb, turbine units; TSW, temporary spillway weir; Bays, area spill bays. The (/) denotes the TSW was not installed at this time. Superscripts denote number of transitions used to calculate percentage, a > 100; b = 50 to 100; c = 10 to 50; (*) = < 10, which was insufficient sample size to calculate percentage]

| | PH #1 | | PH #2 | | PH #3 | | SP #1 | | | SP #2 | SP #3 | |
| | | | | | | | Area of Passage | | | | | |
Species	JBS	Turbine	JBS	Turbine	JBS	Turbine	TSW 22	TSW 20	Bays	Bays	Bays	TSW 4
YCH	13^a	1^a	15^a	5^a	15^a	9^a	/	/	87^a	10^c	*	/
STH	7^a	3^a	7^a	2^a	4^a	3^a	/	/	44^a	21^b	57^c	/
SCH	15^a	10^a	10^a	12^a	7^a	13^a	/	/	54^b	55^c	93^c	/

Table 22. Percentage of fish passing McNary Dam during night period in 2006 based on a one-step Markov Chain analysis.

[Data represent all fish that first approached the powerhouse during the night period. Species: YCH, Yearling Chinook salmon; STH, juvenile steelhead; SCH, subyearling Chinook salmon. Area of Passage: PH#1, turbine units 1–5; PH#2, turbine units 6–10; PH#3, turbine units 11–14; SP#1, spill bays 16–22; SP#2, spill bays 1–6; SP#3, spill bays 7–15; SP#2, spill bays 1–6; JBS, juvenile bypass system; Turb, turbine units; TSW, temporary spillway weir; Bays, area spill bays. The (/) denotes the TSW was not installed at this time. Superscripts denote number of transitions used to calculate percentage, a > 100; b = 50 to 100; c = 10 to 50; (*) = < 10, which was insufficient sample size to calculate percentage]

| | PH #1 | | PH #2 | | PH #3 | | SP #1 | | | SP #2 | SP #3 | |
| | | | | | | | Area of Passage | | | | | |
Species	JBS	Turbine	JBS	Turbine	JBS	Turbine	TSW 22	TSW 20	Bays	Bays	Bays	TSW 4
YCH	24^a	9^a	21^a	10^a	21^a	15^a	/	/	83^c	*	*	/
STH	12^a	3^a	4^a	2^a	4^a	2^a	/	/	27^a	16^a	42^b	/
SCH	6^a	10^a	4^a	10^a	3^a	5^a	/	/	38^b	31^c	95^c	/

Table 23. Percentage of fish passing McNary Dam during day period in 2007 based on a one-step Markov Chain analysis.

[Data represent all fish that first approached the powerhouse during the day period. Species: YCH, Yearling Chinook salmon; STH, juvenile steelhead; SCH, subyearling Chinook salmon. Area of Passage: PH#1, turbine units 1–5; PH#2, turbine units 6–10; PH#3, turbine units 11–14; SP#1, spill bays 16–22; SP#2, spill bays 7–15; SP#3, spill bays 1–6; JBS, juvenile bypass system; Turb, turbine units; TSW, temporary spillway weir; Bays, area spill bays. The (/) denotes the TSW was not installed at this time. Superscripts denote number of transitions used to calculate percentage, a > 100; b = 50 to 100; c = 10 to 50; (*) = < 10, which was insufficient sample size to calculate percentage]

| | | | | | | | Area of Passage | | | | | | |
| | PH #1 | | PH #2 | | PH #3 | | SP #1 | | | SP #2 | SP #3 | |
Species	JBS	Turbine	JBS	Turbine	JBS	Turbine	TSW 22	TSW 20	Bays	Bays	Bays	TSW 4
YCH	16^a	5^a	25^a	3^a	10^a	9^a	75^a	9^a	7^a	27^c	*	/
STH	2^a	1^a	2^a	0^a	1^a	1^a	69^a	10^a	3^a	0^b	6^c	/
SCH	24^a	5^a	23^a	4^a	5^a	11^a	61^a	12^a	13^a	*	*	/

Table 24. Percentage of fish passing McNary Dam during night period in 2007 based on a one-step Markov Chain analysis.

[Data represent all fish that first approached the powerhouse during the night period. Species: YCH, Yearling Chinook salmon; STH, juvenile steelhead; SCH, subyearling Chinook salmon. Area of Passage: PH#1, turbine units 1–5; PH#2, turbine units 6–10; PH#3, turbine units 11–14; SP#1, spill bays 16–22; SP#2, spill bays 7–15; SP#3, spill bays 1–6; JBS, juvenile bypass system; Turb, turbine units; TSW, temporary spillway weir; Bays, area spill bays. The (/) denotes the TSW was not installed at this time. Superscripts denote number of transitions used to calculate percentage, a > 100; b = 50 to 100; c = 10 to 50; (*) = < 10, which was insufficient sample size to calculate percentage]

| | | | | | | | Area of Passage | | | | | | |
| | PH #1 | | PH #2 | | PH #3 | | SP #1 | | | SP #2 | SP #3 | |
Species	JBS	Turbine	JBS	Turbine	JBS	Turbine	TSW 22	TSW 20	Bays	Bays	Bays	TSW 4
YCH	22^a	3^a	23^a	3^a	13^a	4^a	75^b	4^b	15^b	*	*	/
STH	7^a	2^a	6^a	0^a	7^a	0^a	40^a	13^a	7^a	3^b	38^c	/
SCH	9^a	6^a	9^a	6^a	4^a	6^a	45^b	15^b	13^b	25^c	*	/

40

Table 25. Percentage of fish passing McNary Dam during day period in 2008 based on a one-step Markov Chain analysis.

[Data represent all fish that first approached the powerhouse during the day period. Species: YCH, Yearling Chinook salmon; STH, juvenile steelhead; SCH, subyearling Chinook salmon. Area of Passage: PH#1, turbine units 1–5; PH#2, turbine units 6–10; PH#3, turbine units 11–14; SP#1, spill bays 16–22; SP#2, spill bays 7–15; SP#3, spill bays 1–6; JBS, juvenile bypass system; Turb, turbine units; TSW, temporary spillway weir; Bays, area spill bays. The (/) denotes the TSW was not installed at this time. Superscripts denote number of transitions used to calculate percentage, a > 100; b = 50 to 100; c = 10 to 50; (*) = < 10, which was insufficient sample size to calculate percentage]

	PH #1		PH #2		PH #3		SP #1			SP #2	SP #3	
Species	JBS	Turbine	JBS	Turbine	JBS	Turbine	TSW 20	TSW 19	Bays	Bays	Bays	TSW 4
YCH	11^a	6^a	17^a	8^a	11^a	10^a	32^b	14^b	39^b	*	*	/
STH	7^a	1^a	3^a	1^a	3^a	5^a	45^a	19^a	14^a	8^c	*	/
SCH	10^a	12^a	6^a	13^a	2^a	13^a	18^a	14^a	46^a	37^c	*	/

Table 26. Percentage of fish passing McNary Dam during night period in 2008 based on a one-step Markov Chain analysis.

[Data represent all fish that first approached the powerhouse during the night period. Species: YCH, Yearling Chinook salmon; STH, juvenile steelhead; SCH, subyearling Chinook salmon. Area of Passage: PH#1, turbine units 1–5; PH#2, turbine units 6–10; PH#3, turbine units 11–14; SP#1, spill bays 16–22; SP#2, spill bays 7–15; SP#3, spill bays 1–6; JBS, juvenile bypass system; Turb, turbine units; TSW, temporary spillway weir; Bays, area spill bays. The (/) denotes the TSW was not installed at this time. Superscripts denote number of transitions used to calculate percentage, a > 100; b = 50 to 100; c = 10 to 50; (*) = < 10, which was insufficient sample size to calculate percentage]

	PH #1		PH #2		PH #3		SP #1			SP #2	SP #3	
Species	JBS	Turbine	JBS	Turbine	JBS	Turbine	TSW 20	TSW 19	Bays	Bays	Bays	TSW 4
YCH	21^b	5^b	10^a	7^a	9^b	9^b	31^c	14^c	16^c	18^c	*	/
STH	13^a	4^a	9^a	2^a	6^a	6^a	27^a	9^a	17^a	11^c	50^c	/
SCH	14^a	10^a	7	5^a	2^b	12^b	22^b	18^b	18^b	20^c	*	/

Table 27. Percentage of fish passing McNary Dam during day period in 2009 based on a one-step Markov Chain analysis.

[Data represent all fish that first approached the powerhouse during the day period. Species: YCH, Yearling Chinook salmon; STH, juvenile steelhead; SCH, subyearling Chinook salmon. Area of Passage: PH#1, turbine units 1–5; PH#2, turbine units 6–10; PH#3, turbine units 11–14; SP#1, spill bays 16–22; SP#2, SP#3, spill bays 7–15; SP#2, spill bays 1–6; JBS, juvenile bypass system; Turb, turbine units; TSW, temporary spillway weir; Bays, area spill bays. The (\\) denotes the TSW was not installed at this time. Superscripts denote number of transitions used to calculate percentage, a > 100; b = 50 to 100; c = 10 to 50; (*) = < 10, which was insufficient sample size to calculate percentage]

	PH #1		PH #2		PH #3		SP #1			SP #2	SP #3	
Species	JBS	Turbine	JBS	Turbine	JBS	Turbine	TSW 20	TSW 19	Bays	Bays	Bays	TSW 4
YCH	17[a]	4[a]	11[a]	5[a]	20[a]	9[a]	20[a]	\\	57[a]	53[c]	*	*
STH	7[a]	0[a]	5[a]	2[a]	4[a]	1[a]	43[a]	\\	20[a]	6[b]	12[c]	39[c]
SCH	11[a]	7[a]	5[a]	6[a]	14[a]	14[a]	31[a]	5[a]	32[a]	43[b]	57[c]	0[c]

Area of Passage

Table 28. Percentage of fish passing McNary Dam during night period in 2009 based on a one-step Markov Chain analysis.

[Data represent all fish that first approached the powerhouse during the night period. Species: YCH, Yearling Chinook salmon; STH, juvenile steelhead; SCH, subyearling Chinook salmon. Area of Passage: PH#1, turbine units 1–5; PH#2, turbine units 6–10; PH#3, turbine units 11–14; SP#1, spill bays 16–22; SP#2, SP#3, spill bays 7–15; SP#2, spill bays 1–6; JBS, juvenile bypass system; Turb, turbine units; TSW, temporary spillway weir; Bays, area spill bays. The (\\) denotes the TSW was not installed at this time. Superscripts denote number of transitions used to calculate percentage, a > 100; b = 50 to 100; c = 10 to 50; (*) = < 10, which was insufficient sample size to calculate percentage]

	PH #1		PH #2		PH #3		SP #1			SP #2	SP #3	
Species	JBS	Turbine	JBS	Turbine	JBS	Turbine	TSW 20	TSW 19	Bays	Bays	Bays	TSW 4
YCH	12[a]	6[a]	13[a]	5[a]	18[a]	7[a]	24[b]	\\	37[b]	40[c]	*	*
STH	10[a]	2[a]	8[a]	2[a]	8[a]	1[a]	20[a]	\\	13[a]	18[a]	20[b]	26[b]
SCH	7[a]	8[a]	4[a]	8[a]	15[a]	16[a]	33[a]	13[a]	26[a]	26[c]	65[c]	0[c]

Area of Passage

Transition Probabilities during Day and Night for Fish that First Approached the Spillway.

There were no consistent patterns between day and night passage probabilities for fish that first approached the spillway. In 2006, passage proportions for yearling Chinook salmon in the SP#1 area during the night were higher compared to the day and the opposite was observed for steelhead and subyearling Chinook salmon (tables 29 and 30). The relatively low number of transitions (10–50) used to calculate the passage probabilities in 2006 for subyearling Chinook salmon in the SP#1 area could have contributed to these inconsistent results.

In 2007, sample sizes were higher, and the results were more consistent, perhaps because of the installation of the TSWs. Of the fish that entered the SP#1 area, a higher proportion of all three species passed this area during the day compared to night, more so for steelhead (tables 31 and 32). This same pattern was observed during 2008 and 2009 (tables 33, 34, 35, and 36).

For the fish that first approached the spillway, the proportion of fish that passed the powerhouse areas during the day versus the night did not reveal consistent trends. The relatively low number of transitions (10–50) used to generate the passage probabilities in the powerhouse areas likely contributed to the variability in the results.

Two-Step Markov Chain Results

The results from the two-step analysis are presented in the following sections. The main difference between the one-step and two-step analysis is fish location before it transitioned and passed the dam. For example, table 37 shows the passage probabilities of fish passing McNary Dam during 2006 based on a two-step analysis. In this example, 0.34 of the steelhead that entered the SP#1 area passed through the SP#1 area after first transitioning from the PH#3 area. Only 0.21 of the steelhead that entered the SP#1 area passed through that area after first transitioning from the SP#2 area. The two-step analysis allowed us to investigate how passage probabilities were influenced by where the fish was located before it transitioned into and passed one of the six areas upstream of the dam.

Transition Probabilities Regardless of where Fish First Approached the Dam

During 2006, the highest passage probabilities within each of the three powerhouse areas were observed for fish that had transitioned into each area from the forebay, not the adjoining areas to the north or south (table 37). This trend was not constant in the spillway areas. In the SP#1 area, the highest passage proportions where observed for yearling and subyearling Chinook salmon that had been previously observed in the PH#3 area. About the same proportion of steelhead passed the SP#1 area after transitioning from the forebay or the PH#3 areas. Of the fish that passed the SP#3 area, passage probabilities were much higher for fish that had been previously observed in the SP#2 area compared to fish that had been previously observed in the forebay.

The addition of the TSWs during 2007 in the SP#1 area changed the trends that were observed in the powerhouse and spillway. For yearling Chinook salmon, the highest passage probabilities within each of the three powerhouse areas were observed for fish that had transitioned into each area from the forebay (table 38). This trend was not observed for steelhead or subyearling Chinook salmon.

Table 29. Percentage of fish passing McNary Dam during day period in 2006 based on a one-step Markov Chain analysis.

[Data represent all fish that first approached the spillway during the day period. Species: YCH, Yearling Chinook salmon; STH, juvenile steelhead; SCH, subyearling Chinook salmon. Area of Passage: PH#1, turbine units 1–5; PH#2, turbine units 6–10; PH#3, turbine units 11–14; SP#1, spill bays 16–22; SP#2, spill bays 7–15; SP#3, spill bays 1–6; JBS, juvenile bypass system; Turb, turbine units; TSW, temporary spillway weir; Bays, area spill bays. The (\) denotes the TSW was not installed at this time. Superscripts denote number of transitions used to calculate percentage, a > 100; b = 50 to 100; c = 10 to 50; (*) = <10, which was insufficient sample size to calculate percentage]

| | PH #1 | | PH #2 | | PH #3 | | SP #1 | | | SP #2 | SP #3 | |
| | | Area of Passage | | | | | | | | | | |
Species	JBS	Turbine	JBS	Turbine	JBS	Turbine	TSW 22	TSW 20	Bays	Bays	Bays	TSW 4
YCH	*	*	25^c	6^c	11^c	0^c	—	—	68^b	45^a	56^b	—
STH	0^c	14^c	3^c	3^c	0^c	3^c	—	—	36^b	26^b	62^c	—
SCH	3^c	13^c	0^b	6^b	2^b	2^b	—	—	26^b	24^c	60^c	—

Table 30. Percentage of fish passing McNary Dam during night period in 2006 based on a one-step Markov Chain analysis.

[Data represent all fish that first approached the spillway during the night period. Species: YCH, Yearling Chinook salmon; STH, juvenile steelhead; SCH, subyearling Chinook salmon. Area of Passage: PH#1, turbine units 1–5; PH#2, turbine units 6–10; PH#3, turbine units 11–14; SP#1, spill bays 16–22; SP#2, spill bays 7–15; SP#3, spill bays 1–6; JBS, juvenile bypass system; Turb, turbine units; TSW, temporary spillway weir; Bays, area spill bays. The (\) denotes the TSW was not installed at this time. Superscripts denote number of transitions used to calculate percentage, a > 100; b = 50 to 100; c = 10 to 50; (*) = <10, which was insufficient sample size to calculate percentage]

| | PH #1 | | PH #2 | | PH #3 | | SP #1 | | | SP #2 | SP #3 | |
| | | Area of Passage | | | | | | | | | | |
Species	JBS	Turbine	JBS	Turbine	JBS	Turbine	TSW 22	TSW 20	Bays	Bays	Bays	TSW 4
YCH	*	*	*	*	*	*	—	—	82^b	59^a	60^b	—
STH	16^c	2^c	4^b	1^b	8^b	0^b	—	—	22^a	23^a	41^b	—
SCH	10^c	14^c	0^c	6^c	0^c	0^c	—	—	14^c	32^c	62^c	—

44

Table 31. Percentage of fish passing McNary Dam during day period in 2007 based on a one-step Markov Chain analysis.

[Data represent all fish that first approached the spillway during the day period. Species: YCH, Yearling Chinook salmon; STH, juvenile steelhead; SCH, subyearling Chinook salmon. Area of Passage: PH#1, turbine units 1–5; PH#2, turbine units 6–10; PH#3, turbine units 11–14; SP#1, spill bays 16–22; SP#2, spill bays 7–15; SP#3, spill bays 1–6; JBS, juvenile bypass system; Turb, turbine units; TSW, temporary spillway weir; Bays, area spill bays. The (\) denotes the TSW was not installed at this time. Superscripts denote number of transitions used to calculate percentage, a > 100; b = 50 to 100; c = 10 to 50; (*) = <10, which was insufficient sample size to calculate percentage]

| | | | | | | | Area of Passage | | | | | |
| | PH #1 | | PH #2 | | PH #3 | | SP #1 | | | SP #2 | SP #3 | |
Species	JBS	Turbine	JBS	Turbine	JBS	Turbine	TSW 22	TSW 20	Bays	Bays	Bays	TSW 4
YCH	10^c	0^c	33^c	5^c	8^c	11^c	18^a	21^a	40^a	40^a	22^c	\
STH	6^b	4^b	1^b	0^b	1^a	1^a	24^a	27^a	16^a	6^a	0^c	\
SCH	36^c	0^c	21^c	0^c	0^c	17^c	20^b	27^b	30^b	19^c	*	\

Table 32. Percentage of fish passing McNary Dam during night period in 2007 based on a one-step Markov Chain analysis.

[Data represent all fish that first approached the spillway during the night period. Species: YCH, Yearling Chinook salmon; STH, juvenile steelhead; SCH, subyearling Chinook salmon. Area of Passage: PH#1, turbine units 1–5; PH#2, turbine units 6–10; PH#3, turbine units 11–14; SP#1, spill bays 16–22; SP#2, spill bays 7–15; SP#3, spill bays 1–6; JBS, juvenile bypass system; Turb, turbine units; TSW, temporary spillway weir; Bays, area spill bays. The (\) denotes the TSW was not installed at this time. Superscripts denote number of transitions used to calculate percentage, a > 100; b = 50 to 100; c = 10 to 50; (*) = <10, which was insufficient sample size to calculate percentage]

| | | | | | | | Area of Passage | | | | | |
| | PH #1 | | PH #2 | | PH #3 | | SP #1 | | | SP #2 | SP #3 | |
Species	JBS	Turbine	JBS	Turbine	JBS	Turbine	TSW 22	TSW 20	Bays	Bays	Bays	TSW 4
YCH	*	*	21^c	7^c	0^c	26^c	22^a	17^a	35^a	21^b	27^c	\
STH	4^b	1^b	9^a	0^a	5^b	0^b	24^a	12^a	14^a	12^b	25^c	\
SCH	11^c	0^c	0^c	4^c	14^c	0^c	30^b	26^b	17^b	13^c	20^c	\

Table 33. Percentage of fish passing McNary Dam during day period in 2008 based on a one-step Markov Chain analysis.

[Data represent all fish that first approached the spillway during the day period. Species: YCH, Yearling Chinook salmon; STH, juvenile steelhead; SCH, subyearling Chinook salmon. Area of Passage: PH#1, turbine units 1–5; PH#2, turbine units 6–10; PH#3, turbine units 11–14; SP#1, spill bays 16–22; SP#2, spill bays 7–15; SP#3, spill bays 1–6; JBS, juvenile bypass system; Turb, turbine units; TSW, temporary spillway weir; Bays, area spill bays. The (\) denotes the TSW was not installed at this time. Superscripts denote number of transitions used to calculate percentage, a > 100; b = 50 to 100; c = 10 to 50; (*) = < 10, which was insufficient sample size to calculate percentage]

| | PH #1 | | PH #2 | | PH #3 | | SP #1 | | | SP #2 | SP #3 | |
Species	JBS	Turbine	JBS	Turbine	JBS	Turbine	TSW 20	TSW 19	Bays	Bays	Bays	TSW 4
YCH	0[c]	0[c]	11[c]	0[c]	5[c]	24[c]	16[b]	30[b]	21[b]	8[b]	20[c]	\
STH	3[c]	0[c]	0[c]	0[c]	2[b]	3[b]	18[a]	21[a]	15[a]	3[b]	4[c]	\
SCH	0[c]	4[c]	0[c]	0[c]	0[c]	23[c]	19[b]	17[b]	33[b]	8[c]	*	\

Table 34. Percentage of fish passing McNary Dam during night period in 2008 based on a one-step Markov Chain analysis.

[Data represent all fish that first approached the spillway during the night period. Species: YCH, Yearling Chinook salmon; STH, juvenile steelhead; SCH, subyearling Chinook salmon. Area of Passage: PH#1, turbine units 1–5; PH#2, turbine units 6–10; PH#3, turbine units 11–14; SP#1, spill bays 16–22; SP#2, spill bays 7–15; SP#3, spill bays 1–6; JBS, juvenile bypass system; Turb, turbine units; TSW, temporary spillway weir; Bays, area spill bays. The (\) denotes the TSW was not installed at this time. Superscripts denote number of transitions used to calculate percentage, a > 100; b = 50 to 100; c = 10 to 50; (*) = < 10, which was insufficient sample size to calculate percentage]

| | PH #1 | | PH #2 | | PH #3 | | SP #1 | | | SP #2 | SP #3 | |
Species	JBS	Turbine	JBS	Turbine	JBS	Turbine	TSW 20	TSW 19	Bays	Bays	Bays	TSW 4
YCH	*	*	*	*	13[c]	38[c]	11[c]	28[c]	17[c]	9[c]	25[c]	\
STH	17[c]	0[c]	0[c]	3[c]	5[b]	11[b]	10[b]	14[b]	14[b]	12[b]	5[c]	\
SCH	0[c]	0[c]	0[c]	8[c]	6[c]	18[c]	15[c]	26[c]	26[c]	5[c]	*	\

46

Table 35. Percentage of fish passing McNary Dam during day period in 2009 based on a one-step Markov Chain analysis.

[Data represent all fish that first approached the spillway during the day period. Species: YCH, Yearling Chinook salmon; STH, juvenile steelhead; SCH, subyearling Chinook salmon. Area of Passage: PH#1, turbine units 1–5; PH#2, turbine units 6–10; PH#3, turbine units 11–14; SP#1, spill bays 16–22; SP#2, spill bays 7–15; SP#3, spill bays 1–6; JBS, juvenile bypass system; Turb, turbine units; TSW, temporary spillway weir; Bays, area spill bays. The (\) denotes the TSW was not installed at this time. Superscripts denote number of transitions used to calculate percentage, a > 100; b = 50 to 100; c = 10 to 50; (*) = < 10, which was insufficient sample size to calculate percentage]

		Area of Passage										
	PH #1		PH #2		PH #3		SP #1			SP #2	SP #3	
Species	JBS	Turbine	JBS	Turbine	JBS	Turbine	TSW 20	TSW 19	Bays	Bays	Bays	TSW 4
YCH	15^c	8^c	16^c	8^c	19^b	12^b	21^a	\	32^a	53^a	47^b	23^b
STH	7^c	4^c	10^b	0^b	11^b	1^b	34^a	\	12^a	16^a	19^a	29^a
SCH	0^c	0^c	0^c	8^c	5^c	13^c	18^a	32^a	18^a	54^a	53^b	0^b

Table 36. Percentage of fish passing McNary Dam during night period in 2009 based on a one-step Markov Chain analysis.

[Data represent all fish that first approached the spillway during the night period. Species: YCH, Yearling Chinook salmon; STH, juvenile steelhead; SCH, subyearling Chinook salmon. Area of Passage: PH#1, turbine units 1–5; PH#2, turbine units 6–10; PH#3, turbine units 11–14; SP#1, spill bays 16–22; SP#2, spill bays 7–15; SP#3, spill bays 1–6; JBS, juvenile bypass system; Turb, turbine units; TSW, temporary spillway weir; Bays, area spill bays. The (\) denotes the TSW was not installed at this time. Superscripts denote number of transitions used to calculate percentage, a > 100; b = 50 to 100; c = 10 to 50; (*) = < 10, which was insufficient sample size to calculate percentage]

		Area of Passage										
	PH #1		PH #2		PH #3		SP #1			SP #2	SP #3	
Species	JBS	Turbine	JBS	Turbine	JBS	Turbine	TSW 20	TSW 19	Bays	Bays	Bays	TSW 4
YCH	*	*	30^c	10^c	23^c	20^c	21^a	\	29^a	53^a	34^b	28^b
STH	6^b	1^b	5^a	0^a	15^a	1^a	19^a	\	16^a	32^a	23^a	27^a
SCH	0^c	9^c	0^c	17^c	23^c	26^c	16^a	33^a	9^a	48^a	54^b	0^b

Table 37. Percentage of fish passing McNary Dam during day and night periods in 2006 based on a two-step Markov Chain analysis.

[Data represent all fish regardless of where they first approached the dam and include both day and night periods. Species: YCH, Yearling Chinook salmon; STH, juvenile steelhead; SCH, subyearling Chinook salmon. Area of Passage: PH#1, turbine units 1–5; PH#2, turbine units 6–10; PH#3, turbine units 11–14; SP#1, spill bays 16–22; SP#2, spill bays 7–15; SP#3, spill bays 1–6; Service Bay, equipment service bay on the south end of powerhouse; JBS, juvenile bypass system; Turb, turbine units; TSW, temporary spillway weir; Bays, area spill bays. The (\) denotes the TSW was not installed at this time. Superscripts denote number of transitions used to calculate percentage, a > 100; b = 50 to 100; c = 10 to 50; (*) = < 10, which was insufficient sample size to calculate percentage]

Area of Passage:	PH #1						PH #2					
	passing PH#1 after coming from Service Bay		passing PH#1 after coming from forebay		passing PH#1 after coming from PH#2		passing PH#2 after coming from PH#1		passing PH#2 after coming from forebay		passing PH#2 after coming from PH#3	
Species	JBS	Turb	JBS	Turb	JBS	Turb	JBS	Turb	JBS	Turb	JBS	Turb
YCH	18^a	6^a	32^a	7^a	9^a	2^a	11^a	5^a	34^a	14^a	13^a	4^a
STH	9^b	3^b	22^a	4^a	7^a	2^a	4^a	1^a	15^a	5^a	3^a	1^a
SCH	11^a	12^a	18^a	15^a	8^a	8^a	5^a	11^a	12^a	14^a	7^a	7^a

Area of Passage:	PH #3						SP #1								
	passing PH#3 after coming from PH#2		passing PH#3 after coming from forebay		passing PH#3 after coming from SP#1		passing SP#1 after coming from PH#3			passing SP#1 after coming from forebay			passing SP#1 after coming from SP#2		
Species	JBS	Turb	JBS	Turb	JBS	Turb	TSW 22	TSW 20	Bays	TSW 22	TSW 20	Bays	TSW 22	TSW 20	Bays
YCH	13^a	8^a	26^a	18^a	0^c	6^c	\	\	85^a	\	\	68^b	\	\	81^b
STH	3^a	1^a	11^a	11^a	7^a	1^a	\	\	34^a	\	\	36^b	\	\	21^a
SCH	4^a	7^a	8^a	15^a	2^b	4^b	\	\	48^a	\	\	11^c	\	\	22^c

Area of Passage:	SP #2			SP #3			
	passing SP#2 after coming from SP#1	passing SP#2 after coming from forebay	passing SP#2 after coming from SP#3	passing SP1#3 after coming from SP#2		passing SP#3 after coming from forebay	
Species	Bays	Bays	Bays	Bays	TSW 4	Bays	TSW 4
YCH	51^c	54^a	36^b	65^b	\	54^b	\
STH	20^a	38^b	7^b	50^a	\	36^c	\
SCH	42^a	22^c	9^c	90^b	\	*	\

Table 38. Percentage of fish passing McNary Dam during day and night periods in 2007 based on a two-step Markov Chain analysis.

[Data represent all fish regardless of where they first approached the dam and include both day and night periods. Species: YCH, Yearling Chinook salmon; STH, juvenile steelhead; SCH, subyearling Chinook salmon. Area of Passage: PH#1, turbine units 1–5; PH#2, turbine units 6–10; PH#3, turbine units 11–14; SP#1, spill bays 16–22; SP#2, spill bays 7–15; SP#3, spill bays 1–6; Service Bay, equipment service bay on the south end of powerhouse; JBS, juvenile bypass system; Turb, turbine units; TSW, temporary spillway weir; Bays, area spill bays. The (\) denotes the TSW was not installed at this time. Superscripts denote number of transitions used to calculate percentage, a > 100; b = 50 to 100; c = 10 to 50; (*) = < 10, which was insufficient sample size to calculate percentage]

Area of Passage:	PH #1						PH #2					
	passing PH#1 after coming from Service Bay		passing PH#1 after coming from forebay		passing PH#1 after coming from PH#2		passing PH#2 after coming from PH#1		passing PH#2 after coming from forebay		passing PH#2 after coming from PH#3	
Species	JBS	Turb	JBS	Turb	JBS	Turb	JBS	Turb	JBS	Turb	JBS	Turb
YCH	18[a]	6[a]	27[a]	5[a]	13[a]	2[a]	21[a]	2[a]	33[a]	3[a]	22[a]	4[a]
STH	5[a]	4[a]	6[a]	1[a]	3[a]	1[a]	4[a]	0[a]	4[a]	1[a]	5[a]	0[a]
SCH	13[a]	7[a]	26[a]	7[a]	14[a]	3[a]	13[a]	5[a]	23[a]	4[a]	18[a]	3[a]

Area of Passage:	PH #3						SP #1								
	passing PH#3 after coming from PH#2		passing PH#3 after coming from forebay		passing PH#3 after coming from SP#1		passing SP#1 after coming from PH#3			passing SP#1 after coming from forebay			passing SP#1 after coming from SP#2		
Species	JBS	Turb	JBS	Turb	JBS	Turb	TSW 22	TSW 20	Bays	TSW 22	TSW 20	Bays	TSW 22	TSW 20	Bays
YCH	5[a]	4[a]	18[a]	12[a]	4[b]	21[b]	76[a]	8[a]	7[a]	25[a]	25[a]	29[a]	6[a]	16[a]	54[a]
STH	2[a]	1[a]	7[a]	0[a]	2[a]	1[a]	67[a]	10[a]	2[a]	18[a]	23[a]	9[a]	13[a]	26[a]	23[a]
SCH	5[a]	8[a]	5[a]	10[a]	4[b]	14[b]	56[a]	12[a]	14[a]	28[a]	24[a]	26[a]	6[b]	33[b]	16[b]

Area of Passage:	SP #2			SP #3			
	passing SP#2 after coming from SP#1	passing SP#2 after coming from forebay	passing SP#2 after coming from SP#3	passing SP1#3 after coming from SP#2		passing SP#3 after coming from forebay	
Species	Bays	Bays	Bays	Bays	TSW 4	Bays	TSW 4
YCH	38[c]	34[a]	32[b]	40[c]	\	21[c]	\
STH	5[a]	7[a]	4[b]	18[b]	\	9[c]	\
SCH	28[c]	10[c]	13[c]	60[c]	\	17[c]	\

49

For these two species, the passage probabilities for fish that passed one of the three powerhouse areas was about the same, and relatively low compared to yearling Chinook salmon, regardless of which area they were in before passing the powerhouse. In the spillway, passage probabilities were higher for fish that had been previously observed in the SP#2 area compared to fish that had previously been previously observed in the forebay. Within the SP#1 area, the highest passage probabilities were for fish that passed after transitioning from the PH#3 area. The two-step analysis of the 2007 data also revealed some interesting trends in the passage probabilities through the two TSWs. Of the fish that passed TSW22, the largest proportion had transitioned from the PH#3 area before passing. The PH#3 area is the area closest to the south and adjacent to the area where TSW22 was located. Of the fish that passed through TSW20, very few had been previously observed in the PH#3 area. Instead, of the fish that passed TSW20, the greatest proportion had transitioned from the SP#2 area, the area immediately north of the SP#1 area.

The trends in passage probabilities observed in 2007 also were evident in 2008; however, moving the location of the TSWs within the SP#1 area had a noticeable effect on the proportion of fish passing through the TSWs (table 39). Passage through the SP#1 area was still relatively high compared to 2006, but within the SP#1 area, the proportion of fish passing through the two TSWs decreased and the proportion passing the standard spill bays increased. There was variability in the results among species, but in general, the proportions of fish that passed through the TSWs after transitioning from the PH#3 area decreased. We also observed a general decrease in the proportion of fish passing through the TSWs after transitioning from the SP#2 area. The proportion of fish passing the PH#3 area after transitioning from the SP#1 area increased in 2008, indicating that less fish passed the SP#1 area and instead transitioned into the PH#3 area before passing the dam.

The proportion of fish that passed the SP#1 area after transitioning from either the PH#3 or SP#2 area was affected by having only one TSW located in the SP#1 area during the spring study period of 2009 (table 40). During spring 2009, a TSW was located in bay 20, two bays farther from the powerhouse compared to 2007 and one less TSW in the SP#1 area than 2008, and the second TSW was placed in spill bay 4 (SP#3 area). The added distance between the powerhouse and the first TSW to the north, combined with having only one TSW in that area, likely contributed to the differences in the passage proportion observed in 2009 compared to 2008 and 2007. For yearling Chinook salmon and steelhead in 2009, the proportion of fish that passed through TSW20 after transitioning from the PH#3 area was greater than what was observed in 2008 for TSW20. However, the proportions of fish that passed through TSW20 during 2009 (this was the TSW closest to the powerhouse) were not as high as what was observed in 2007 for TSW22 (located two bays closer to the powerhouse). Although fish passage proportions decreased in the SP#1 area, relocating one of the TSWs to the SP#3 area did positively affect passage probabilities in the SP#3 area. During years when no TSW was located in the SP#3 area, the proportion of fish that passed after entering this area generally was less than 0.50. During the spring of 2009, we observed increased passage in this area compared to previous years and the proportions of spring species that passed after transitioning from the SP#2 area increased (table 40).

Regardless of where fish first approached the dam, there were differences in passage probabilities during the day and night. The trends varied among the three species and across the 4 years included in the analysis. The results of the two-step analysis for all fish regardless of where they first approached the dam during the day and night are presented in appendix C. The effect of diel period on the passage probabilities is discussed in more detail in the section describing transition probabilities during day and night for fish that first approached the powerhouse and first approached the spillway.

Table 39. Percentage of fish passing McNary Dam during day and night periods in 2008 based on a two-step Markov Chain analysis.

[Data represent all fish regardless of where they first approached the dam and include both day and night periods. Species: YCH, Yearling Chinook salmon; STH, juvenile steelhead; SCH, subyearling Chinook salmon. Area of Passage: PH#1, turbine units 1–5; PH#2, turbine units 6–10; PH#3, turbine units 11–14; SP#1, spill bays 16–22; SP#2, spill bays 7–15; SP#3, spill bays 1–6; Service Bay, equipment service bay on the south end of powerhouse; JBS, juvenile bypass system; Turb, turbine units; TSW, temporary spillway weir; Bays, area spill bays. The (\) denotes the TSW was not installed at this time. Superscripts denote number of transitions used to calculate percentage, a > 100; b = 50 to 100; c = 10 to 50; (*) = < 10, which was insufficient sample size to calculate percentage]

Area of Passage:	PH #1						PH #2					
(Service Bay)	passing PH#1 after coming from Service Bay		passing PH#1 after coming from forebay		passing PH#1 after coming from PH#2		passing PH#2 after coming from PH#1		passing PH#2 after coming from forebay		passing PH#2 after coming from PH#3	
Species	JBS	Turb	JBS	Turb	JBS	Turb	JBS	Turb	JBS	Turb	JBS	Turb
YCH	13^c	5^c	17^b	5^b	14^a	4^a	11^a	8^a	22^b	4^b	11^b	8^b
STH	7^b	2^b	16^a	5^a	9^a	1^a	7^a	2^a	1^b	1^b	4^a	1^a
SCH	8^a	9^a	19^a	12^a	7^a	11^a	6^a	11^a	8^a	14^a	1^b	2^b

Area of Passage:	PH #3						SP #1								
(PH# 2)	passing PH#3 after coming from PH#2		passing PH#3 after coming from forebay		passing PH#3 after coming from SP#1		passing SP#1 after coming from PH#3			passing SP#1 after coming from forebay			passing SP#1 after coming from SP#2		
Species	JBS	Turb	JBS	Turb	JBS	Turb	TSW 20	TSW 19	Bays	TSW 20	TSW 19	Bays	TSW 20	TSW 19	Bays
YCH	9^a	12^a	11^b	4^b	8^b	31^b	33^a	11^a	27^a	16^b	25^b	20^b	11^b	37^b	22^b
STH	3^a	3^a	6^a	1^a	3^a	15^a	36^a	13^a	16^a	10^b	15^b	10^b	11^a	26^a	15^a
SCH	3^a	11^a	2^b	11^b	0^b	28^b	21^a	14^a	39^a	24^b	15^b	21^b	6^b	28^b	35^b

Area of Passage:	SP #2			SP #3			
(SP# 1)	passing SP#2 after coming from SP#1	passing SP#2 after coming from forebay	passing SP#2 after coming from SP#3	passing SP#3 after coming from SP#2		passing SP#3 after coming from forebay	
Species	Bays	Bays	Bays	Bays	TSW 4	Bays	TSW 4
YCH	7^c	8^b	12^c	31^c	\	15^c	\
STH	10^b	0^c	12^b	21^c	\	6^c	\
SCH	32^c	4^c	0^c	58^c	\	9^c	\

Table 40. Percentage of fish passing McNary Dam during day and night periods in 2009 based on a two-step Markov Chain analysis.

[Data represent all fish regardless of where they first approached the dam and include both day and night periods. Species: YCH, Yearling Chinook salmon; STH, juvenile steelhead; SCH, subyearling Chinook salmon. Area of Passage: PH#1, turbine units 1–5; PH#2, turbine units 6–10; PH#3, turbine units 11–14; SP#1, spill bays 16–22; SP#2, spill bays 7–15; SP#3, spill bays 1–6; Service Bay, equipment service bay on the south end of powerhouse; JBS, juvenile bypass system; Turb, turbine units; TSW, temporary spillway weir; Bays, area spill bays. The (\) denotes the TSW was not installed at this time. Superscripts denote number of transitions used to calculate percentage, a > 100; b = 50 to 100; c = 10 to 50; (*) = < 10, which was insufficient sample size to calculate percentage]

Area of Passage:	PH #1						PH #2					
	passing PH#1 after coming from Service Bay		passing PH#1 after coming from forebay		passing PH#1 after coming from PH#2		passing PH#2 after coming from PH#1		passing PH#2 after coming from forebay		passing PH#2 after coming from PH#3	
Species	JBS	Turb	JBS	Turb	JBS	Turb	JBS	Turb	JBS	Turb	JBS	Turb
YCH	16^a	7^a	19^a	8^a	12^a	3^a	9^a	5^a	23^a	7^a	12^a	3^a
STH	8^a	2^a	9^a	2^a	9^a	1^a	6^a	1^a	13^a	5^a	6^a	1^a
SCH	8^a	6^a	16^a	11^a	5^a	7^a	3^a	6^a	8^a	8^a	4^a	8^a

Area of Passage:	PH #3						SP #1								
	passing PH#3 after coming from PH#2		passing PH#3 after coming from forebay		passing PH#3 after coming from SP#1		passing SP#1 after coming from PH#3			passing SP#1 after coming from forebay			passing SP#1 after coming from SP#2		
Species	JBS	Turb	JBS	Turb	JBS	Turb	TSW 20	TSW 19	Bays	TSW 20	TSW 19	Bays	TSW 20	TSW 19	Bays
YCH	17^a	4^a	24^a	16^a	20^b	15^b	22^a	\	50^a	22^a	\	36^a	18^b	\	20^b
STH	6^a	1^a	14^a	1^a	9^a	2^a	33^a	\	16^a	26^a	\	16^a	21^a	\	15^a
SCH	11^a	11^a	20^a	24^a	22^b	14^b	32^a	7^a	32^a	24^a	27^a	20^a	7^a	44^a	2^a

Area of Passage:	SP #2			SP #3			
	passing SP#2 after coming from SP#1	passing SP#2 after coming from forebay	passing SP#2 after coming from SP#3	passing SP#3 after coming from SP#2		passing SP#3 after coming from forebay	
Species	Bays	Bays	Bays	Bays	TSW 4	Bays	TSW 4
YCH	63^b	52^a	28^c	52^c	29^c	34^b	27^b
STH	21^a	32^a	9^a	21^a	31^a	17^b	24^b
SCH	55^a	47^a	39^b	57^b	0^b	53^a	0^a

Transition Probabilities after First Approaching the Powerhouse

In 2006, a high proportion of fish first approached the powerhouse and passed through the SP#1 area during the day and night periods combined after transitioning from the PH#3 area in the powerhouse. Of the fish transitioning from PH#3 to SP#1, 0.87 of the yearling Chinook salmon, 0.34 of the steelhead, and 0.49 of the subyearling Chinook salmon passed the SP#1 area (table 41). Few fish passing the SP#1 area had transitioned from the adjoining areas in the spillway (SP#2 or SP#3). The proportion of fish that passed within each of the areas in the powerhouse (PH#1, PH#2, and PH#3) after first approaching the powerhouse was higher for fish that transitioned from the forebay compared to fish that transitioned from adjoining areas across the face of the dam before passing.

Similar trends were observed for the powerhouse during 2007 when the TSWs were installed in the SP#1 area. In the spillway, similar to the results of the one-step analysis, the addition of the TSWs increased the proportion of fish passing the SP#1 area, especially for steelhead. The two-step analysis showed a majority of the fish passing the SP#1 area after transitioning from the PH#3 area (table 42). Of the fish that passed the SP#1 area, very few passed after transitioning from the other two areas in the spillway. As was observed in 2006, the proportion of fish that first approached the powerhouse, and then entered and passed the PH#3 area was low for fish that transitioned from the spillway and relatively high for fish that transitioned from the other areas in the powerhouse.

The overall passage trends observed in 2007 also were observed in 2008 and 2009 for fish that first approached the powerhouse (table 43 and 44). Once again, the proportion of the fish that first approached the powerhouse, and then entered and passed the SP#1 area was highest for fish that transitioned from the PH#3 area. However, as was evident from the one-step analysis, moving the locations of the TSWs influenced passage within the SP#1 area. Of the fish that first approached the powerhouse and then passed the SP#1 area during 2007, 0.85 of the yearling Chinook salmon, 0.77 of the steelhead, and 0.69 of the subyearling Chinook salmon passed through the two TSWs in bay 20 and 22 after transitioning from the PH#3 area. Less than 0.13 of the fish passing through the SP#1 area after transitioning from the PH#3 area did so through the other bays within the SP#1 area. In 2008, only 0.46 of the yearling Chinook salmon, 0.50 of the steelhead, and 0.34 of the subyearling Chinook salmon that had transitioned from the PH#3 area passed the two TSWs in bays 20 and 19. The proportion of fish passing through the other bays in the SP#1 area after transitioning from the PH#3 area during 2008 increased to 0.28 for yearling Chinook salmon, 0.16 for steelhead, and 0.39 for subyearling Chinook salmon. In spring 2009, when one TSW was present in the SP#1 area, the number of fish first detected in the powerhouse that entered and passed through the SP#1 area was again highest for fish that transitioned from the PH#3 area, but the proportion of fish that passed through the TSWs decreased and the proportion of fish that passed through the other bays increased.

We conducted further analysis using the two-step methods to investigate how passage proportions for fish that first approach the powerhouse might be influenced if the fish passed during the day compared to the night. The overall trends in passage proportions were similar to those observed for fish regardless of the time of day they passed. The results are presented in appendix D.

Table 41. Percentage of fish passing McNary Dam during day and night periods in 2006 based on a two-step Markov Chain analysis.

[Data represent all fish that first approached the powerhouse and include both day and night periods. Species: YCH, Yearling Chinook salmon; STH, juvenile steelhead; SCH, subyearling Chinook salmon. Area of Passage: PH#1, turbine units 1–5; PH#2, turbine units 6–10; PH#3, turbine units 11–14; SP#1, spill bays 16–22; SP#2, spill bays 7–15; SP#3, spill bays 1–6; Service Bay, equipment service bay on the south end of powerhouse; JBS, juvenile bypass system; Turb, turbine units; TSW, temporary spillway weir; Bays, area spill bays; NA, not applicable. The (\) denotes the TSW was not installed at this time. Superscripts denote number of transitions used to calculate percentage, a > 100; b = 50 to 100; c = 10 to 50; (*) = < 10, which was insufficient sample size to calculate percentage]

Area of Passage:	PH #1						PH #2					
	passing PH#1 after coming from Service Bay		passing PH#1 after coming from forebay		passing PH#1 after coming from PH#2		passing PH#2 after coming from PH#1		passing PH#2 after coming from forebay		passing PH#2 after coming from PH#3	
Species	JBS	Turb	JBS	Turb	JBS	Turb	JBS	Turb	JBS	Turb	JBS	Turb
YCH	18[a]	6[a]	32[a]	7[a]	8[a]	2[a]	11[a]	5[a]	34[a]	14[a]	13[a]	3[a]
STH	10[b]	4[b]	22[a]	4[a]	5[a]	2[a]	4[a]	2[a]	15[a]	5[a]	3[a]	1[a]
SCH	11[a]	11[a]	18[a]	15[a]	8[a]	7[a]	5[a]	11[a]	12[a]	14[a]	8[a]	8[a]

Area of Passage:	PH #3						SP #1								
	passing PH#3 after coming from PH#2		passing PH#3 after coming from forebay		passing PH#3 after coming from SP#1		passing SP#1 after coming from PH#3			passing SP#1 after coming from forebay			passing SP#1 after coming from SP#2		
Species	JBS	Turb	JBS	Turb	JBS	Turb	TSW 22	TSW 20	Bays	TSW 22	TSW 20	Bays	TSW 22	TSW 20	Bays
YCH	12[a]	8[a]	26[a]	18[a]	*	*	\	\	87[a]	NA	NA	NA	\	\	*
STH	3[a]	1[a]	11[a]	11[a]	6[b]	0[b]	\	\	34[a]	NA	NA	NA	\	\	24[b]
SCH	4[a]	8[a]	8[a]	15[a]	8[c]	8[c]	\	\	49[a]	NA	NA	NA	\	\	*

Area of Passage:	SP #2			SP #3			
	passing SP#2 after coming from SP#1	passing SP#2 after coming from forebay	passing SP#2 after coming from SP#3	passing SP#3 after coming from SP#2		passing SP#3 after coming from forebay	
Species	Bays	Bays	Bays	Bays	TSW 4	Bays	TSW 4
YCH	15[c]	NA	*	*	\	NA	NA
STH	20[a]	NA	9[c]	46[b]	\	NA	NA
SCH	44[b]	NA	*	94[c]	\	NA	NA

Table 42. Percentage of fish passing McNary Dam during day and night periods in 2007 based on a two-step Markov Chain analysis.

[Data represent all fish that first approached the powerhouse and include both day and night periods. Species: YCH, Yearling Chinook salmon; STH, juvenile steelhead; SCH, subyearling Chinook salmon. Area of Passage: PH#1, turbine units 1–5; PH#2, turbine units 6–10; PH#3, turbine units 11–14; SP#1, spill bays 16–22; SP#2, spill bays 7–15; SP#3, spill bays 1–6; Service Bay, equipment service bay on the south end of powerhouse; JBS, juvenile bypass system; Turb, turbine units; TSW, temporary spillway weir; Bays, area spill bays; NA, not applicable. The (\) denotes the TSW was not installed at this time. Superscripts denote number of transitions used to calculate percentage, a > 100; b = 50 to 100; c = 10 to 50; (*) = < 10, which was insufficient sample size to calculate percentage]

Area of Passage:	PH #1						PH #2					
	passing PH#1 after coming from Service Bay		passing PH#1 after coming from forebay		passing PH#1 after coming from PH#2		passing PH#2 after coming from PH#1		passing PH#2 after coming from forebay		passing PH#2 after coming from PH#3	
Species	JBS	Turb	JBS	Turb	JBS	Turb	JBS	Turb	JBS	Turb	JBS	Turb
YCH	17^a	7^a	27^a	5^a	14^a	2^a	21^a	2^a	33^a	3^a	22^a	4^a
STH	5^a	3^a	6^a	1^a	3^a	1^a	3^a	0^a	4^a	1^a	4^a	0^a
SCH	13^a	8^a	26^a	7^a	14^a	3^a	13^a	6^a	23^a	4^a	19^a	3^a

Area of Passage:	PH #3						SP #1								
	passing PH#3 after coming from PH#2		passing PH#3 after coming from forebay		passing PH#3 after coming from SP#1		passing SP#1 after coming from PH#3			passing SP#1 after coming from forebay			passing SP#1 after coming from SP#2		
Species	JBS	Turb	JBS	Turb	JBS	Turb	TSW 22	TSW 20	Bays	TSW 22	TSW 20	Bays	TSW 22	TSW 20	Bays
YCH	5^a	4^a	18^a	12^a	*	*	78^a	7^a	7^a	NA	NA	NA	*	*	*
STH	2^a	1^a	7^a	0^a	3^b	0^b	67^a	10^a	2^a	NA	NA	NA	10^b	20^b	15^b
SCH	5^a	8^a	6^a	9^a	0^c	25^c	56^a	13^a	13^a	NA	NA	NA	*	*	*

Area of Passage:	SP #2			SP #3			
	passing SP#2 after coming from SP#1	passing SP#2 after coming from forebay	passing SP#2 after coming from SP#3	passing SP#3 after coming from SP#2		passing SP#3 after coming from forebay	
Species	Bays	Bays	Bays	Bays	TSW 4	Bays	TSW 4
YCH	31^c	NA	*	*	\	NA	NA
STH	1^b	NA	3^c	25^c	\	NA	NA
SCH	30^c	NA	*	*	\	NA	NA

Table 43. Percentage of fish passing McNary Dam during day and night periods in 2008 based on a two-step Markov Chain analysis.

[Data represent all fish that first approached the powerhouse and include both day and night periods. Species: YCH, Yearling Chinook salmon; STH, juvenile steelhead; SCH, subyearling Chinook salmon. Area of Passage: PH#1, turbine units 1–5; PH#2, turbine units 6–10; PH#3, turbine units 11–14; SP#1, spill bays 16–22; SP#2, spill bays 7–15; SP#3, spill bays 1–6; Service Bay, equipment service bay on the south end of powerhouse; JBS, juvenile bypass system; Turb, turbine units; TSW, temporary spillway weir; Bays, area spill bays; NA, not applicable. The (\) denotes the TSW was not installed at this time. Superscripts denote number of transitions used to calculate percentage, a > 100; b = 50 to 100; c = 10 to 50; (*) = < 10, which was insufficient sample size to calculate percentage]

Area of Passage:	PH #1						PH #2					
	passing PH#1 after coming from Service Bay		passing PH#1 after coming from forebay		passing PH#1 after coming from PH#2		passing PH#2 after coming from PH#1		passing PH#2 after coming from forebay		passing PH#2 after coming from PH#3	
Species	JBS	Turb	JBS	Turb	JBS	Turb	JBS	Turb	JBS	Turb	JBS	Turb
YCH	14^c	5^c	17^b	5^b	14^b	5^b	11^a	8^a	22^b	4^b	12^b	10^b
STH	6^b	2^b	16^a	5^a	10^a	1^a	9^a	3^a	1^b	1^b	6^a	0^a
SCH	9^a	9^a	19^a	12^a	8^a	12^a	7^a	11^a	8^a	14^a	2^b	3^b

Area of Passage:	PH #3						SP #1								
	passing PH#3 after coming from PH#2		passing PH#3 after coming from forebay		passing PH#3 after coming from SP#1		passing SP#1 after coming from PH#3			passing SP#1 after coming from forebay			passing SP#1 after coming from SP#2		
Species	JBS	Turb	JBS	Turb	JBS	Turb	TSW 20	TSW 19	Bays	TSW 20	TSW 19	Bays	TSW 20	TSW 19	Bays
YCH	9^a	12^a	12^b	4^b	15^c	23^c	35^a	11^a	28^a	NA	NA	NA	0^c	42^c	33^c
STH	3^a	4^a	6^a	1^a	4^b	21^b	38^a	12^a	16^a	NA	NA	NA	21^c	38^c	8^c
SCH	3^a	12^a	2^b	12^b	0^c	25^c	20^a	14^a	39^a	NA	NA	NA	0^c	23^c	23^c

Area of Passage:	SP #2			SP #3			
	passing SP#2 after coming from SP#1	passing SP#2 after coming from forebay	passing SP#2 after coming from SP#3	passing SP#3 after coming from SP#2		passing SP#3 after coming from forebay	
Species	Bays	Bays	Bays	Bays	TSW 4	Bays	TSW 4
YCH	13^c	NA	*	*	\	NA	NA
STH	14^c	NA	0^c	44^c	\	NA	NA
SCH	33^c	NA	*	64^c	\	NA	NA

Table 44. Percentage of fish passing McNary Dam during day and night periods in 2009 based on a two-step Markov Chain analysis.

[Data represent all fish that first approached the powerhouse and include both day and night periods. Species: YCH, Yearling Chinook salmon; STH, juvenile steelhead; SCH, subyearling Chinook salmon. Area of Passage: PH#1, turbine units 1–5; PH#2, turbine units 6–10; PH#3, turbine units 11–14; SP#1, spill bays 16–22; SP#2, spill bays 7–15; SP#3, spill bays 1–6; Service Bay, equipment service bay on the south end of powerhouse; JBS, juvenile bypass system; Turb, turbine units; TSW, temporary spillway weir; Bays, area spill bays; NA, not applicable. The (\) denotes the TSW was not installed at this time. Superscripts denote number of transitions used to calculate percentage, a > 100; b = 50 to 100; c = 10 to 50; (*) = < 10, which was insufficient sample size to calculate percentage]

Area of Passage:	PH #1						PH #2					
	passing PH#1 after coming from Service Bay		passing PH#1 after coming from forebay		passing PH#1 after coming from PH#2		passing PH#2 after coming from PH#1		passing PH#2 after coming from forebay		passing PH#2 after coming from PH#3	
Species	JBS	Turb	JBS	Turb	JBS	Turb	JBS	Turb	JBS	Turb	JBS	Turb
YCH	16^a	6^a	19^a	8^a	12^a	3^a	9^a	5^a	23^a	7^a	10^a	3^a
STH	9^a	2^a	9^a	2^a	9^a	1^a	5^a	1^a	13^a	5^a	6^a	1^a
SCH	8^a	6^a	16^a	11^a	5^a	7^a	3^a	6^a	8^a	8^a	4^a	7^a

Area of Passage:	PH #3						SP #1								
	passing PH#3 after coming from PH#2		passing PH#3 after coming from forebay		passing PH#3 after coming from SP#1		passing SP#1 after coming from PH#3			passing SP#1 after coming from forebay			passing SP#1 after coming from SP#2		
Species	JBS	Turb	JBS	Turb	JBS	Turb	TSW 20	TSW 19	Bays	TSW 20	TSW 19	Bays	TSW 20	TSW 19	Bays
YCH	16^a	4^a	24^a	16^a	31^c	6^c	22^a	\	50^a	NA	\	NA	*	\	*
STH	5^a	1^a	13^a	1^a	2^b	2^b	33^a	\	16^a	NA	\	NA	18^b	\	16^b
SCH	11^a	10^a	20^a	24^a	27^c	4^c	33^a	7^a	31^a	NA	NA	NA	6^c	38^c	0^c

Area of Passage:	SP #2			SP #3			
	passing SP#2 after coming from SP#1	passing SP#2 after coming from forebay	passing SP#2 after coming from SP#3	passing SP1#3 after coming from SP#2		passing SP#3 after coming from forebay	
Species	Bays	Bays	Bays	Bays	TSW 4	Bays	TSW 4
YCH	47^c	NA	*	42^c	50^c	NA	NA
STH	16^a	NA	12^b	17^a	30^a	NA	NA
SCH	39^b	NA	27^c	61^c	0^c	NA	NA

Transition Probabilities after First Approaching the Spillway

The two-step analysis of fish that first approached the spillway during the day and night periods combined indicated that powerhouse passage after lateral movement of fish from the spillway to PH#3 was relatively low for all species. During 2006, of the fish that first approached the spillway, 0.11 or less (depending on species) of the fish transitioning from SP#1 to PH#3 passed in the PH#3 area (table 45). During 2007, lateral movement from the spillway to the powerhouse for fish that passed the PH#3 area was still relatively low at 0.25 or less, depending on species (table 46). In contrast, the number of fish that passed the SP#1 area after transitioning from the powerhouse area (PH#3) was much greater in 2007 than in 2006. In 2006, 0.40 or less of the fish passed the SP#1 area after transitioning from the PH#3 area. With the addition of the TSWs in 2007, 0.89 of the yearling Chinook salmon, 0.71 of the steelhead, and 0.80 of the subyearling Chinook salmon passed the SP#1 area after transitioning from the PH#3 area. During 2008, the proportion of fish that passed the SP#1 area after transitioning from the powerhouse was again higher than observed in 2006, but less than what was observed in 2007 (table 47). This was likely the result of moving the locations of the TSWs in 2008. Having only one TSW in the SP#1 area during the spring of 2009 may have resulted in more lateral movement within and between the powerhouse and spillway before fish passed. During 2009, the number of fish passing the SP#1 area after transitioning from the PH#3 area increased for yearling Chinook salmon and decreased for steelhead (table 48). Similarly, the number of fish passing the PH#1 and PH#2 area after moving from one of the adjoining powerhouse areas increased in 2009 compared to 2008.

We conducted further analysis using the two-step methods to investigate how passage proportions for fish that first approach the spillway might be influenced if the fish passed during the day compared to the night. The overall trends in passage proportions were similar to those observed for fish regardless of the time of day they passed. The results are presented in appendix E.

Table 45. Percentage of fish passing McNary Dam during day and night periods in 2006 based on a two-step Markov Chain analysis.

[Data represent all fish that first approached the spillway and include both day and night periods. Species: YCH, Yearling Chinook salmon; STH, juvenile steelhead; SCH, subyearling Chinook salmon. Area of Passage: PH#1, turbine units 1–5; PH#2, turbine units 6–10; PH#3, turbine units 11–14; SP#1, spill bays 16–22; SP#2, spill bays 7–15; SP#3, spill bays 1–6; Service Bay, equipment service bay on the south end of powerhouse; JBS, juvenile bypass system; Turb, turbine units; TSW, temporary spillway weir; Bays, area spill bays; NA, not applicable. The (\) denotes the TSW was not installed at this time. Superscripts denote number of transitions used to calculate percentage, a > 100; b = 50 to 100; c = 10 to 50; (*) = < 10, which was insufficient sample size to calculate percentage]

Area of Passage:	PH #1						PH #2					
	passing PH#1 after coming from Service Bay		passing PH#1 after coming from forebay		passing PH#1 after coming from PH#2		passing PH#2 after coming from PH#1		passing PH#2 after coming from forebay		passing PH#2 after coming from PH#3	
Species	JBS	Turb	JBS	Turb	JBS	Turb	JBS	Turb	JBS	Turb	JBS	Turb
YCH	*	*	NA	NA	*	*	*	*	NA	NA	25^c	6^c
STH	0^c	0^c	NA	NA	15^c	6^c	5^c	0^c	NA	NA	3^b	2^b
SCH	7^c	13^c	NA	NA	7^c	13^c	0^c	6^c	NA	NA	0^b	6^b

Area of Passage:	PH #3						SP #1								
	passing PH#3 after coming from PH#2		passing PH#3 after coming from forebay		passing PH#3 after coming from SP#1		passing SP#1 after coming from PH#3			passing SP#1 after coming from forebay			passing SP#1 after coming from SP#2		
Species	JBS	Turb	JBS	Turb	JBS	Turb	TSW 22	TSW 20	Bays	TSW 22	TSW 20	Bays	TSW 22	TSW 20	Bays
YCH	20^c	0^c	NA	NA	0^c	0^c	\	\	*	\	\	68^b	\	\	84^b
STH	3^b	0^b	NA	NA	9^b	2^b	\	\	32^c	\	\	36^b	\	\	17^b
SCH	3^c	0^c	NA	NA	0^c	3^c	\	\	40^c	\	\	11^c	\	\	25^c

Area of Passage:	SP #2			SP #3			
	passing SP#2 after coming from SP#1	passing SP#2 after coming from forebay	passing SP#2 after coming from SP#3	passing SP1#3 after coming from SP#2		passing SP#3 after coming from forebay	
Species	Bays	Bays	Bays	Bays	TSW 4	Bays	TSW 4
YCH	73^c	54^a	36^b	64^b	\	54^b	\
STH	20^b	38^b	5^c	56^b	\	36^c	\
SCH	36^c	22^c	*	80^c	\	*	\

Table 46. Percentage of fish passing McNary Dam during day and night periods in 2007 based on a two-step Markov Chain analysis.

[Data represent all fish that first approached the spillway and include both day and night periods. Species: YCH, Yearling Chinook salmon; STH, juvenile steelhead; SCH, subyearling Chinook salmon. Area of Passage: PH#1, turbine units 1–5; PH#2, turbine units 6–10; PH#3, turbine units 11–14; SP#1, spill bays 16–22; SP#2, spill bays 7–15; SP#3, spill bays 1–6; Service Bay, equipment service bay on the south end of powerhouse; JBS, juvenile bypass system; Turb, turbine units; TSW, temporary spillway weir; Bays, area spill bays; NA, not applicable. The (\) denotes the TSW was not installed at this time. Superscripts denote number of transitions used to calculate percentage, a > 100; b = 50 to 100; c = 10 to 50; (*) = < 10, which was insufficient sample size to calculate percentage]

Area of Passage:	PH #1						PH #2					
	passing PH#1 after coming from Service Bay		passing PH#1 after coming from forebay		passing PH#1 after coming from PH#2		passing PH#2 after coming from PH#1		passing PH#2 after coming from forebay		passing PH#2 after coming from PH#3	
Species	JBS	Turb	JBS	Turb	JBS	Turb	JBS	Turb	JBS	Turb	JBS	Turb
YCH	*	*	NA	NA	0^c	0^c	*	*	NA	NA	33^c	7^c
STH	6^c	9^c	NA	NA	4^a	0^a	5^b	0^b	NA	NA	5^a	0^a
SCH	*	*	NA	NA	19^c	0^c	5^c	5^c	NA	NA	13^c	0^c

Area of Passage:	PH #3						SP #1								
	passing PH#3 after coming from PH#2		passing PH#3 after coming from forebay		passing PH#3 after coming from SP#1		passing SP#1 after coming from PH#3			passing SP#1 after coming from forebay			passing SP#1 after coming from SP#2		
Species	JBS	Turb	JBS	Turb	JBS	Turb	TSW 22	TSW 20	Bays	TSW 22	TSW 20	Bays	TSW 22	TSW 20	Bays
YCH	8^c	0^c	NA	NA	4^c	21^c	72^c	6^c	11^c	25^a	25^a	29^a	6^a	16^a	53^a
STH	5^b	0^b	NA	NA	1^a	1^a	60^b	10^b	1^b	19^a	22^a	9^a	15^a	28^a	26^a
SCH	9^c	9^c	NA	NA	6^c	9^c	53^c	7^c	20^c	27^a	25^a	26^a	7^c	39^c	17^c

Area of Passage:	SP #2			SP #3			
	passing SP#2 after coming from SP#1	passing SP#2 after coming from forebay	passing SP#2 after coming from SP#3	passing SP1#3 after coming from SP#2		passing SP#3 after coming from forebay	
Species	Bays	Bays	Bays	Bays	TSW 4	Bays	TSW 4
YCH	42^c	34^a	33^c	33^c	\	21^c	\
STH	11^b	7^a	5^b	5^c	\	9^c	\
SCH	27^c	10^c	15^c	*	\	17^c	\

Table 47. Percentage of fish passing McNary Dam during day and night periods in 2008 based on a two-step Markov Chain analysis.

[Data represent all fish that first approached the spillway and include both day and night periods. Species: YCH, Yearling Chinook salmon; STH, juvenile steelhead; SCH, subyearling Chinook salmon. Area of Passage: PH#1, turbine units 1–5; PH#2, turbine units 6–10; PH#3, turbine units 11–14; SP#1, spill bays 16–22; SP#2, spill bays 7–15; SP#3, spill bays 1–6; Service Bay, equipment service bay on the south end of powerhouse; JBS, juvenile bypass system; Turb, turbine units; TSW, temporary spillway weir; Bays, area spill bays; NA, not applicable. The (\) denotes the TSW was not installed at this time. Superscripts denote number of transitions used to calculate percentage, a > 100; b = 50 to 100; c = 10 to 50; (*) = < 10, which was insufficient sample size to calculate percentage]

Area of Passage:	PH #1						PH #2					
	passing PH#1 after coming from Service Bay		passing PH#1 after coming from forebay		passing PH#1 after coming from PH#2		passing PH#2 after coming from PH#1		passing PH#2 after coming from forebay		passing PH#2 after coming from PH#3	
Species	JBS	Turb	JBS	Turb	JBS	Turb	JBS	Turb	JBS	Turb	JBS	Turb
YCH	*	*	NA	NA	13^c	0^c	15^c	8^c	NA	NA	9^c	0^c
STH	20^c	0^c	NA	NA	5^c	0^c	0^c	0^c	NA	NA	0^b	2^b
SCH	0^c	5^c	NA	NA	0^c	0^c	0^c	6^c	NA	NA	0^c	0^c

Area of Passage:	PH #3						SP #1								
	passing PH#3 after coming from PH#2		passing PH#3 after coming from forebay		passing PH#3 after coming from SP#1		passing SP#1 after coming from PH#3			passing SP#1 after coming from forebay			passing SP#1 after coming from SP#2		
Species	JBS	Turb	JBS	Turb	JBS	Turb	TSW 20	TSW 19	Bays	TSW 20	TSW 19	Bays	TSW 20	TSW 19	Bays
YCH	14^c	14^c	NA	NA	5^c	33^c	17^c	8^c	17^c	16^b	25^b	20^b	12^b	36^b	21^b
STH	5^c	0^c	NA	NA	3^b	10^b	27^b	16^b	16^b	10^b	15^b	10^b	8^b	22^b	17^b
SCH	7^c	7^c	NA	NA	0^c	27^c	17^c	17^c	44^c	24^b	15^b	21^b	7^c	29^c	39^c

Area of Passage:	SP #2			SP #3			
	passing SP#2 after coming from SP#1	passing SP#2 after coming from forebay	passing SP#2 after coming from SP#3	passing SP1#3 after coming from SP#2		passing SP#3 after coming from forebay	
Species	Bays	Bays	Bays	Bays	TSW 4	Bays	TSW 4
YCH	0^c	8^b	14^c	36^c	\	15^c	\
STH	6^c	0^c	15^c	4^c	\	6^c	\
SCH	*	4^c	0^c	*	\	9^c	\

Table 48. Percentage of fish passing McNary Dam during day and night periods in 2009 based on a two-step Markov Chain analysis.

[Data represent all fish that first approached the spillway and include both day and night periods. Species: YCH, Yearling Chinook salmon; STH, juvenile steelhead; SCH, subyearling Chinook salmon. Area of Passage: PH#1, turbine units 1–5; PH#2, turbine units 6–10; PH#3, turbine units 11–14; SP#1, spill bays 16–22; SP#2, spill bays 7–15; SP#3, spill bays 1–6; Service Bay, equipment service bay on the south end of powerhouse; JBS, juvenile bypass system; Turb, turbine units; TSW, temporary spillway weir; Bays, area spill bays; NA, not applicable. The (\) denotes the TSW was not installed at this time. Superscripts denote number of transitions used to calculate percentage, a > 100; b = 50 to 100; c = 10 to 50; (*) = < 10, which was insufficient sample size to calculate percentage]

Area of Passage	PH #1						PH #2					
	passing PH#1 after coming from Service Bay		passing PH#1 after coming from forebay		passing PH#1 after coming from PH#2		passing PH#2 after coming from PH#1		passing PH#2 after coming from forebay		passing PH#2 after coming from PH#3	
Species	JBS	Turb	JBS	Turb	JBS	Turb	JBS	Turb	JBS	Turb	JBS	Turb
YCH	*	*	NA	NA	18^c	12^c	0^c	9^c	NA	NA	24^c	8^c
STH	5^c	2^c	NA	NA	7^b	2^b	7^b	0^b	NA	NA	7^a	0^a
SCH	0^c	0^c	NA	NA	0^c	9^c	0^c	10^c	NA	NA	0^c	11^c

Area of Passage	PH #3						SP #1								
	passing PH#3 after coming from PH#2		passing PH#3 after coming from forebay		passing PH#3 after coming from SP#1		passing SP#1 after coming from PH#3			passing SP#1 after coming from forebay			passing SP#1 after coming from SP#2		
Species	JBS	Turb	JBS	Turb	JBS	Turb	TSW 20	TSW 19	Bays	TSW 20	TSW 19	Bays	TSW 20	TSW 19	Bays
YCH	33^c	6^c	NA	NA	17^b	17^b	25^c	\	50^c	22^a	\	36^a	19^b	\	20^b
STH	13^b	0^b	NA	NA	14^a	2^a	34^b	\	11^b	26^a	\	16^a	23^a	\	14^a
SCH	0^c	17^c	NA	NA	19^c	19^c	14^c	19^c	38^c	24^a	27^a	20^a	7^a	45^a	2^a

Area of Passage	SP #2			SP #3			
	passing SP#2 after coming from SP#1	passing SP#2 after coming from forebay	passing SP#2 after coming from SP#3	passing SP1#3 after coming from SP#2		passing SP#3 after coming from forebay	
Species	Bays	Bays	Bays	Bays	TSW 4	Bays	TSW 4
YCH	73^b	52^a	29^c	56^c	22^c	34^b	27^b
STH	34^b	32^a	8^a	25^a	31^a	17^b	24^b
SCH	70^b	47^a	42^b	55^b	0^b	53^a	0^a

Discussion

Prior to conducting the Markov chain analysis there had been limited attempts to establish method to quantify the qualitative information that had been collected on the behavior of juvenile salmonids passing McNary Dam. In the past, the behavior of fish in the forebay was presented in a format that displayed the movements of each fish in three dimensions within a virtual rendition of the forebay of the dam. Most readers of this report will be familiar with the "fish track movies" using the Eonfusion[TM] software that has been used in the past to display this information. That format allowed interested parties to observe virtually how fish moved in different areas across the face of the dam and to examine how fish behavior might differ by species, time of day, passage route, or in response to the installation of a new passage alternative like the TSW. While this was, and still is, a useful way to visualize the data, there was no convenient way to numerically summarize the information. The Markov chain analysis allowed us to numerically summarize the behavior of fish in the forebay.

Numerically summarizing the behavior of juvenile salmonids in the forebay of McNary Dam using the Markov chain analysis allowed us to confirm what previously had been subjectively summarized using the Eonfusion[TM] visualization software. For example, within the powerhouse region, passage proportions among the three areas (PH#1, PH#2, and PH#3) was often greater in the south and middle areas of the powerhouse compared to the northern area of the powerhouse for yearling and subyearling Chinook salmon. The opposite generally was observed for steelhead. The passage probabilities through all three areas in the powerhouse was lower for steelhead compared to the Chinook salmon, and the proportion of steelhead passing through the northern area was consistently lower than the passage proportions in the middle and southern areas. These results confirmed that steelhead, which migrate closer to the surface of the water than Chinook salmon, did not pass readily into the deeper passage routes in the powerhouse. Similar reasoning can be used to explain why the Chinook salmon passage proportions in the powerhouse were higher than the passage proportions for steelhead. Chinook salmon tend to travel deeper in the water and are more likely to enter the deeper passage routes in the powerhouse. The higher passage proportions in the northern area of the powerhouse for Chinook salmon, compared to steelhead, could have been influenced by turbine operations. In most years, the turbines in this area were operated relatively high compared to the rest of the powerhouse (Adams and Liedtke, 2009), which might have resulted in an increased proportion of Chinook salmon passing the powerhouse routes in the PH#3 area. Project operations also may have influenced passage in the spillway. During 2006, planned spill treatment tests resulted in more water passing the bays in the SP#3 area compared to the SP#2 area. This could explain why passage probabilities were higher in the SP#3 area compared to the SP#2 area for all species during 2006.

The results of this analysis also allowed us to confirm and quantify the extent of milling behavior that was observed for steelhead. For fish that were first detected in the powerhouse region, less than 0.10 of the steelhead, on average, passed within each of the powerhouse areas. Instead, steelhead transitioned to adjoining areas before passing the dam. In comparison, greater than 0.20 of the Chinook salmon passed within the powerhouse areas. Less milling behavior was observed for all species for fish that first approached the spillway. Compared to the powerhouse areas, a higher proportion of fish, regardless of species, passed the spillway areas and fewer transitioned to adjoining areas. This was evident in 2006, when no TSW was installed in the spillway, and was more pronounced in subsequent years when TSWs were installed in the spillway. The surface oriented passage routes created by the TSWs resulted in more fish passage and less milling in the spillway areas.

In addition to quantifying what had been previously speculated about the behavior of fish in the forebay of McNary Dam, the Markov chain analysis refined our understanding of how fish behavior and passage can be influenced by changes to the operations and structure of McNary Dam. For example, the addition of TSWs to the spillway area clearly influenced the passage of fish. Previous results have been reported showing that TSWs increased passage through non-turbine routes and the fish-track videos indicated, in general, how fish behaved before passing the temporary spillway weirs (TSWs). However, the analysis presented in this report allowed us to better understand how fish transitioned across the face of the dam before passing the TSWs and resulted in a quantitative way to measure the effect of moving the location of the TSWs from year to year. Installation of the TSWs in bays 22 and 20 clearly increased passage proportions through the spillway #1 (SP#1) area for all species, most significantly for steelhead. When the TSWs were moved to bays 19 and 20 in 2008, overall passage through the SP#1 area remained higher than 2006, but decreased from what was observed in 2007. Shifting the TSWs to the north decreased the proportion of fish passing through the TSWs and increased the number of fish that transitioned to adjoining areas before passing the dam. During spring 2009, when one TSW was moved from SP#1 area to spillway #3 (SP#3) area (bay 4), passage proportions were lower than during 2007 and 2008. The added distance between the powerhouse and the first TSW to the north, combined with having only one TSW in that area (SP#1), likely contributed to the decreased passage proportions in 2009. Although fish passage proportions decreased in the SP#1 area, relocating one of the TSWs to the SP#3 area did positively affect passage probabilities in the SP#3 area. During years when no TSW was located in the SP#3 area, the proportion of fish that passed after entering this area generally was less than 0.50. During the spring of 2009, we observed increased passage in this area compared to previous years and the proportions of spring species that passed after transitioning from the spillway #2 (SP#2) area increased.

Our results showed that it was feasible to use a one-step Markov analyses to quantify fish behavior and the results of the analysis comported well with what has been previously reported in the annual reports of research. The two-step analysis, however, resulted in quantitative information about the behavior of fish that has not been previously reported. For example, of the fish that passed the three areas in the powerhouse, the highest passage proportions were observed for fish that had transitioned from the forebay before passing. This indicated that fish were more likely to pass the powerhouse on their first approach and less likely to pass the powerhouse after transitioning laterally along the powerhouse. It is plausible that the depth at which fish approached the powerhouse contributed to this trend. Perhaps the proportion of the population within each species that migrated deeper passed the powerhouse on their first approach and the fish that migrated shallower approached the powerhouse and moved laterally before passing. This theory can be supported by the differences we observed between species. The proportion of steelhead passing the three powerhouse areas after transitioning from the forebay was lower than what was observed for the Chinook salmon species. If a smaller proportion of the steelhead population is deep in the water column as they approach the dam, then less of the fish would pass through the deeper passage routes in the powerhouse on their first approach to the dam. This passage trend was not consistent in the spillway areas.

In the spillway, the proportion of fish that passed each of the areas after transitioning from the forebay was nearly equal, and sometimes less than, the proportion of fish that passed after transitioning laterally from one of the adjoining areas across the face of the dam. This was particularly evident in the SP#1 area. For yearling Chinook salmon, the proportion of fish that passed the SP#1 area after coming from the PH#3 area was higher than the proportion of fish passing the SP#1 area after coming from the forebay. A similar trend was observed for subyearling Chinook salmon that passed the SP#1 area after coming from the PH#3 area compared to the fish that passed the SP#1 area after coming from the forebay. For steelhead, the proportion of fish that passed the SP#1 are after coming from the forebay was about the same as the proportion of fish that passed the SP#1 area after coming from the powerhouse #3 (PH#3) area. The two-step analysis revealed that the addition of the TSWs in 2007 and 2008 increased passage proportions in the SP#1 area, but the trends in passage proportions relative to where fish transitioned from before passing, did not change from what was observed in 2006. Once again, the proportion of fish passing the SP#1 area after coming from the forebay was lower than the proportion of fish passing the SP#1 area after coming from the PH#3 area.

Perhaps the most interesting new information to come out of the two-step analysis relates to how the performance of the TSWs was influenced by their proximity to the powerhouse. During 2007, the highest proportion of fish passing through TSW22 was from fish that transitioned from the PH#3 area. In contrast, a relatively low proportion of fish passed through TSW20 after coming from the PH#3 area. Instead, the proportion of fish that passed TSW20 after coming from the SP#3 area was twice as high as the proportion of fish that passed through TSW20 after coming from PH#3. During 2008, the TSW in bay 22 was moved to bay 19, leaving the TSW in bay 20 as the one closest to the powerhouse. As was the case when a TSW was located in bay 22, the proportion of fish passing TSW20 after coming from the PH#3 area was greater than the proportion of fish passing TSW20 after coming from the SP#2 area. Passage proportions for fish passing through the TSW in bay 19, the farthest north of the two TSW during 2008, was higher for fish that came from the SP#2 area compared to the proportion of fish that passed through TSW19 after coming from the PH#3 area.

The Markov chain analysis provided a mathematical way to describe fish behavior in the forebay of McNary Dam and helped refine our understanding of how fish movements were influenced by operational and structural changes. In addition, numerical information on the behavior of fish can be used to construct simulations to examine how future proposed structural and operational changes at McNary Dam might influence passage of juvenile salmonids. For example, the data can be used to evaluate how a virtual passage alternative (VPA) located upstream of turbine units 11–14 (PH#3 area) might influence the passage probabilities of juvenile salmonids. To accomplish this, a VPA can be incorporated into the Markov chain analysis as an additional passage route, similar to the juvenile bypass system (JBS) and turbines. Assumptions regarding the efficiency of the VPA can be used in the simulations to estimate the passage proportions through a VPA. For example, the simulation could be used to estimate passage proportions through a VPA that is 10, 30, or 50 percent efficient as a passage alternative. This type of analysis could be used to estimate how efficient a VPA would have to be to make a significant impact to the passage proportions, and ultimately, the survival of fish passing McNary Dam. Simulations of this type can be used to estimate the performance of a VPA before committing the resources to build, install, and test these relatively expensive structures. Constructing and running simulations like this was beyond the scope of this report. However, an example of this type of analysis will be presented in a subsequent report that is scheduled for publication in 2012.

Acknowledgments

We thank Ann Setter, Brad Eby, Bill Prewitt, and individuals in the U.S. Army Corps of Engineers for their cooperation and assistance on the project. We are especially grateful to Rosanna Mensik and individuals working for the Washington Department of Fish and Wildlife for their assistance in collecting fish for the studies. We also greatly appreciate the U.S. Coast Guard, the U.S. Fish and Wildlife Service, the Portland District of the U.S. Army Corps of Engineers, and the Washington Department of Transportation for permission to install acoustic telemetry equipment on their property. We thank all of our colleagues at the Columbia River Research Laboratory for their assistance and dedication. Funding for this project was provided by the U.S. Army Corps of Engineers, Walla Walla District, Washington; Contract W68SBV93504107.

References Cited

Adams, N.S., and Counihan, T.D., eds., 2009, Survival and migration behavior of juvenile salmonids at McNary Dam, 2007: Final report of research prepared by U.S. Geological Survey, Cook, Washington, for the U.S. Army Corps of Engineers, Walla Walla District, Contract W68SBV70178419, Walla Walla, Washington.

Adams, N.S., and Evans, S.D., eds., 2011, Summary of juvenile salmonid passage and survival at McNary Dam—Acoustic survival studies, 2006–09: U.S. Geological Survey Open-File Report 2011–1179, 144 p.

Adams, N.S., and Liedtke, T.L., eds., 2009, Juvenile salmonid survival, passage, and egress at McNary Dam during tests of temporary spillway weirs, 2008: Final report of research prepared by U.S. Geological Survey, Cook, Washington, for the U.S. Army Corps of Engineers, Walla Walla District, Contract W68SBV80448890, Walla Walla, Washington.

Adams, N.S., and Liedtke, T.L., eds., 2010, Juvenile salmonid survival, passage, and egress at McNary Dam during tests of temporary spillway weirs, 2009: Final report of research prepared by U.S. Geological Survey, Cook, Washington, for the U.S. Army Corps of Engineers, Walla Walla District, Contract W68SBV90070150, Walla Walla, Washington.

Adams, N.S., Plumb, J.M., Hatton, T.W., Jones, E.C., Swyers, N.M., Sholtis, M.D., Reagan, R.E., and Cash, K.M., 2008, Survival and migration behavior of juvenile salmonids at McNary Dam, 2006: Final report of research prepared by U.S. Geological Survey, Cook, Washington, for the U.S. Army Corps of Engineers, Walla Walla District, Contract W68SBV60478899, Walla Walla, Washington.

Adams, N.S., Rondorf, D.W, Evans, S.D., Kelly, J.E., and Perry, R.W., 1998, Effects of surgically and gastrically implanted radio transmitters on growth and feeding behavior of juvenile Chinook salmon: Transactions of the American Fisheries Society, v. 127, p. 128–136.

Adams, N.S., Walker, C.E, and Perry, R.W., 2011, A multi-year analysis of passage and survival at McNary Dam, 2004–09: U.S. Geological Survey Open-File Report 2011–1230, 128 p.

Axel, G.A., Hockersmith, E.E., Eppard, M.B., and Sanford, B.P., 2004a, Passage and survival of hatchery yearling Chinook salmon at McNary Dam, 2002: Report by National Marine Fisheries Service to U.S. Army Corps of Engineers, Walla Walla District, Contract W68SBV92844866, Walla Walla, Washington.

Axel, G.A., Hockersmith, E.E., Eppard, M.B., and Sanford, B.P., 2004b, Passage and survival of hatchery yearling Chinook salmon at McNary Dam, 2003: Report by National Marine Fisheries Service to U.S. Army Corps of Engineers, Walla Walla District, Contract W68SBV92844866, Walla Walla, Washington.

Beeman, J.W., Fielding, S.D., Braatz, A.C., Wilkerson, T.S., Pope, A.C., Walker, C.E., Hardiman, J.M., Perry, R.W., and Counihan, T.D., 2007, Survival and migration behavior of juvenile salmonids at Lower Granite Dam, 2006: Final report of research by the U. S. Geological Survey to the U.S. Army Corps of Engineers, Walla Walla District, Contract W68SBV60378208, Walla Walla, Washington.

Johnson, G.E., Hedgepeth, J.B., Skalski, J.R., Giorgi, A.E., 2004, A Markov chain analysis of fish movements to determine entrainment zones: Fisheries Research, v. 69, 349–358.

Perry, R.W., Braatz, A.C., Fielding, S.D., Lucchesi, J.N., Plumb, J.M., Adams, N.S., and Rondorf, D.W., 2006, Survival and migration behavior of juvenile salmonids at McNary Dam, 2004: Final report of research prepared by U.S. Geological Survey, Cook, Washington, for the U.S. Army Corps of Engineers, Walla Walla District, Contract W68SBV40271050, Walla Walla, Washington.

Perry, R.W., Braatz, A.C., Novick, M.S., Lucchesi, J.N., Rutz, G.L., Koch, R.C., Schei, J.S., Adams, N.S., and Rondorf, D.W., 2007a, Survival and migration behavior of juvenile salmonids at McNary Dam, 2005: Final report of research prepared by U.S. Geological Survey, Cook, Washington, for the U.S. Army Corps of Engineers, Walla Walla District, W68SBV50407617, Walla Walla, Washington.

Perry, R.W., Kock, T.J., Novick, M.S., Braatz, A.C., Fielding, S.D., Hansen, G.S., Sprando, J.M., Wilkerson, T.S., George, G.T., Schei, J.L., Adams, N.S., and Rondorf, D.W., 2007b, Survival and migration behavior of juvenile salmonids at Lower Granite Dam, 2005: Final report of research prepared by U.S. Geological Survey, Cook, Washington, for the U.S. Army Corps of Engineers, Walla Walla District, Contract W68SBV50498133, Walla Walla, Washington.

Plumb, J.M., Braatz, A.C., Lucchesi, J.N., Fielding, S.D., Cochran, A.D., Nation, T.K., Sprando, J.M., Schei, J.L., Perry, R.W., Adams, N.S., and Rondorf, D.W., 2004, Behavior and survival of radio-tagged juvenile Chinook salmon and steelhead relative to the performance of a removable spillway weir at Lower Granite Dam, Washington, 2003: Final report of research prepared by U.S. Geological Survey, Cook, Washington, for the U.S. Army Corps of Engineers, Walla Walla District, Contract W68SBV00104592, Walla Walla, Washington.

Puls, A.L., Counihan, T.D, Walker, C.E., Hardiman, J.M., and Duran, I.N., 2008, Survival and migration behavior of subyearling Chinook salmon at Lower Granite Dam, 2007: Final report of research prepared by U.S. Geological Survey, Cook, Washington, for the U.S. Army Corps of Engineers, Walla Walla District, Contract W68SBV70198655, Walla Walla, Washington.

Stewart, W. J. and Stewart J., 1994, Introduction to the numerical solution of Markov chains: Princeton, N.J., Princeton University Press, 539 p.

Skalski, J.R., Townsend, R., Lady, J., Giorgi, A.E., Stevenson, J.R., and McDonald, R.S., 2002, Estimating route-specific passage and survival probabilities at a hydroelectric project from smolt radio telemetry studies: Canadian Journal of Fisheries and Aquatic Sciences, v. 59, p. 1385–1393.

Steel, E., Guttorp, P., Anderson, J., Caccia, D., 2001, Modeling juvenile salmon migration using a simple Markov chain: Journal of Agriculture, Biological and Environmental Statistics, v. 6, p. 80–88.

Glossary

Forebay	Area of Columbia River extending from McNary Dam to 2 km upstream.
Near Dam	Area of Columbia River extending from McNary Dam to approximately 160 m upstream; the area monitored by hydrophones placed from the upstream face of McNary Dam to 60 m upstream, including an average detection range of 100 m.
PIT	Passive integrated transponder.
Powerhouse	Turbine and bypass (units 1–14).
RKM	River kilometer.
SCH	Subyearling Chinook salmon (*Oncorhynchus tshawytscha*).
Spillway	Conventional spill bays (bays 1–22 excluding bays 20 and 22 in 2007, 19 and 20 in 2008, 4 and 20 in spring 2009, and 19 and 20 in summer 2009).
STH	Steelhead (*Oncorhynchus mykiss*).
Tailrace	Area of Columbia River extending from McNary Dam to 2.4 km downstream.
TSW	Temporary spillway weir.
USGS	United States Geological Survey.
YCH	Yearling Chinook salmon (*Oncorhynchus tshawytscha*).

Appendix A. Locations of Hydrophones in the McNary Dam Forebay, 2006–09.

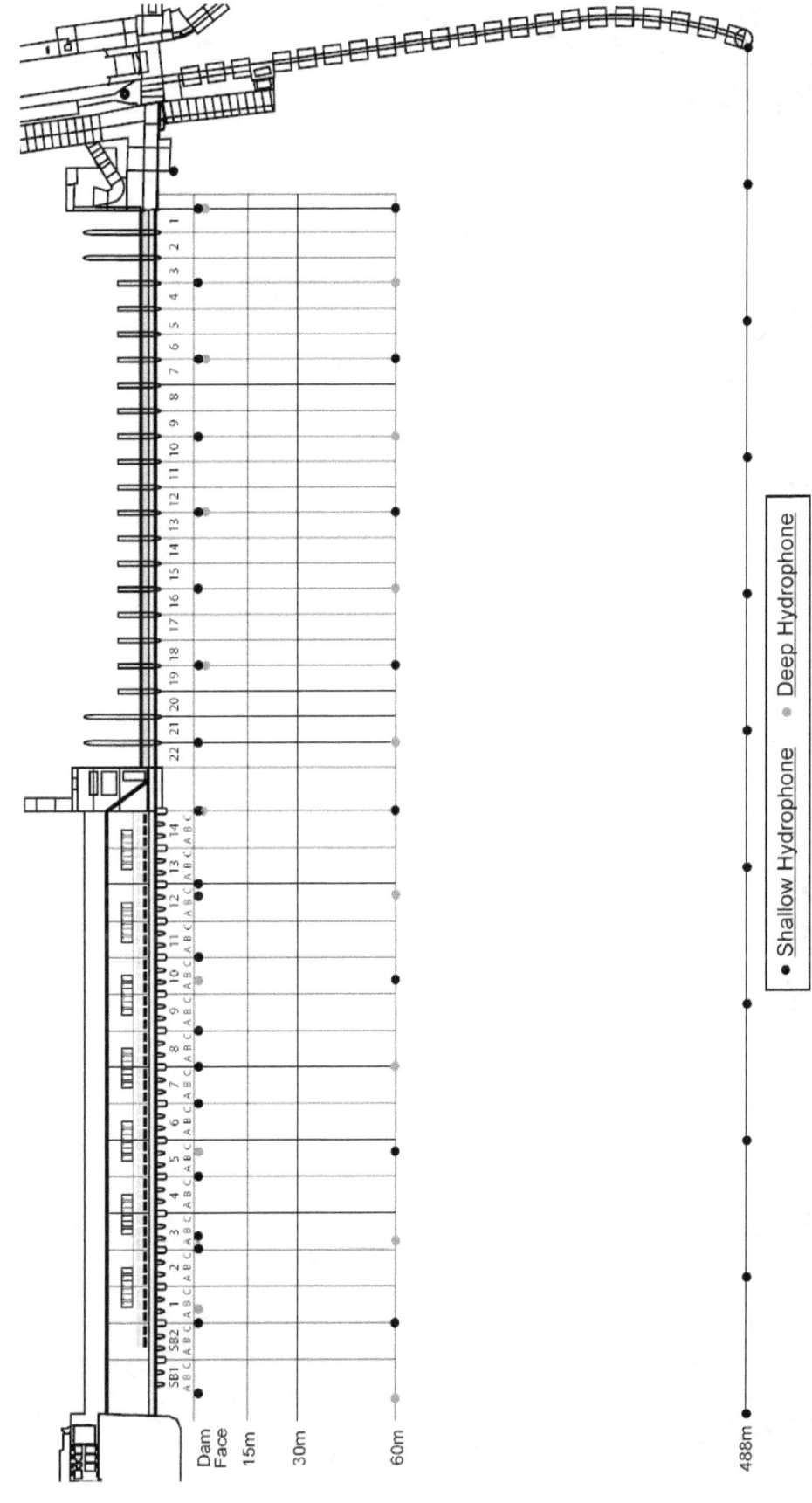

Figure A1. Schematic of hydrophones in the McNary Dam forebay during 2006.

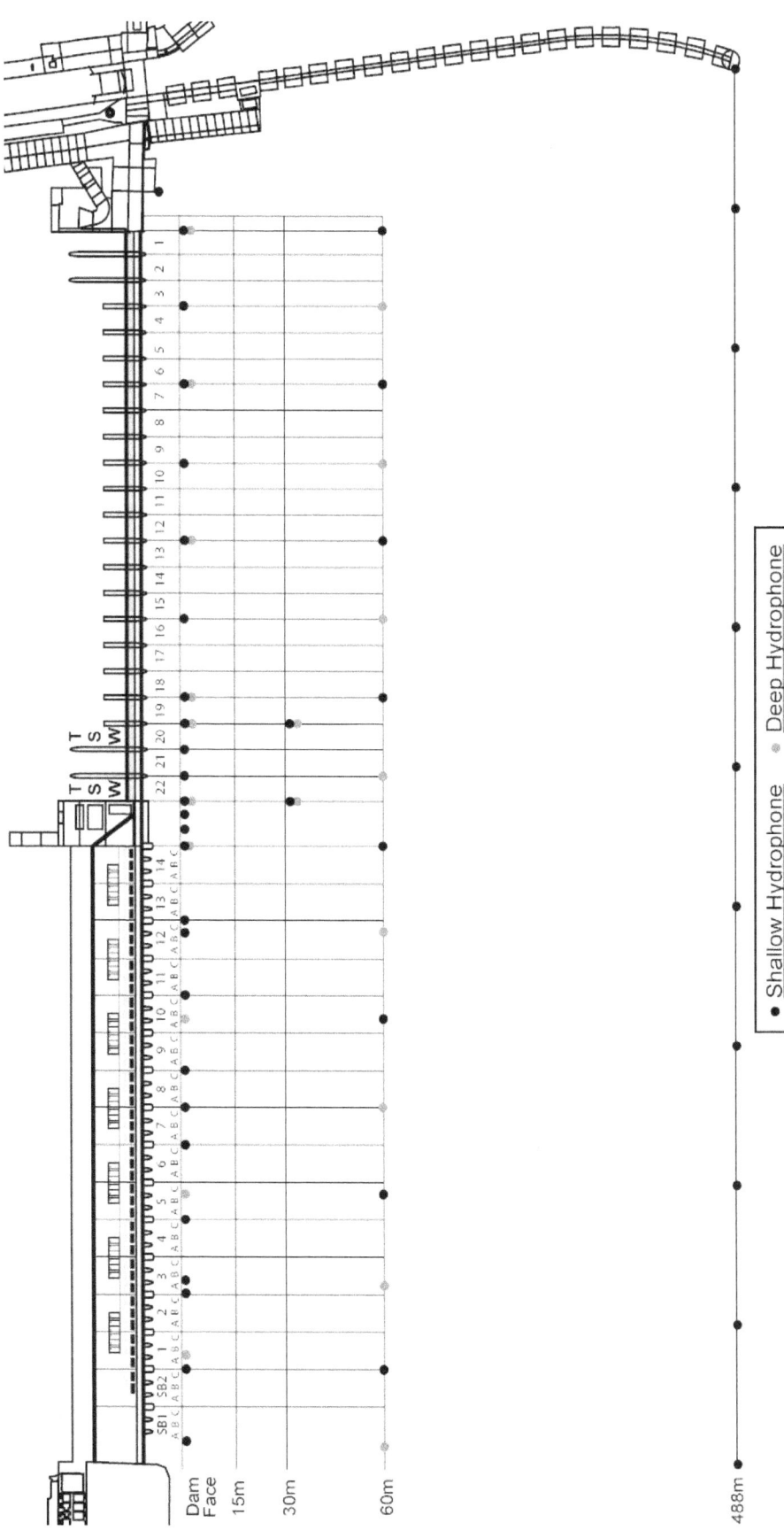

Figure A2. Schematic of hydrophones in the McNary Dam forebay during 2007.

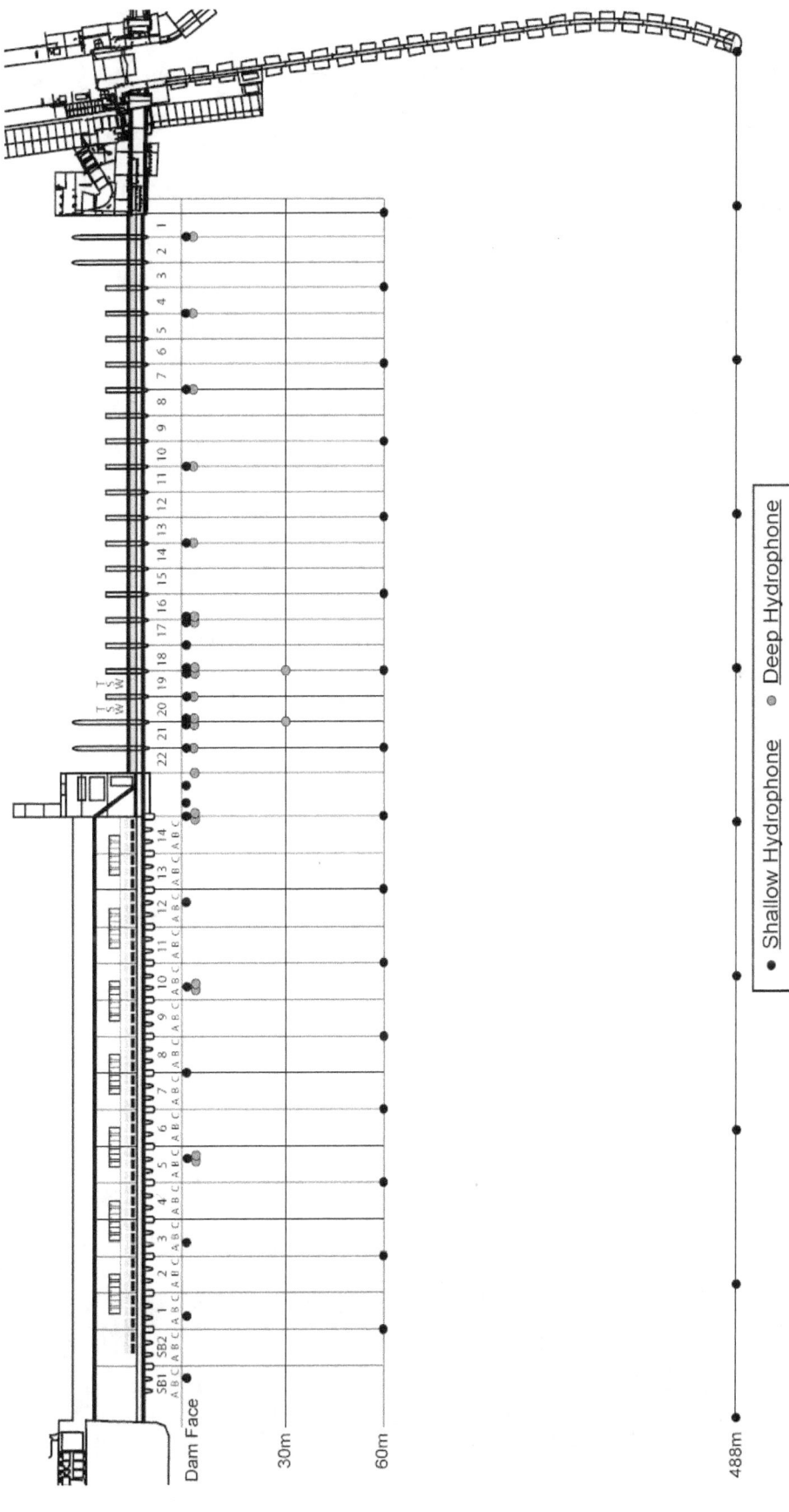

Figure A3. Schematic of hydrophones in the McNary Dam forebay during 2008.

● Shallow Hydrophone ● Deep Hydrophone

71

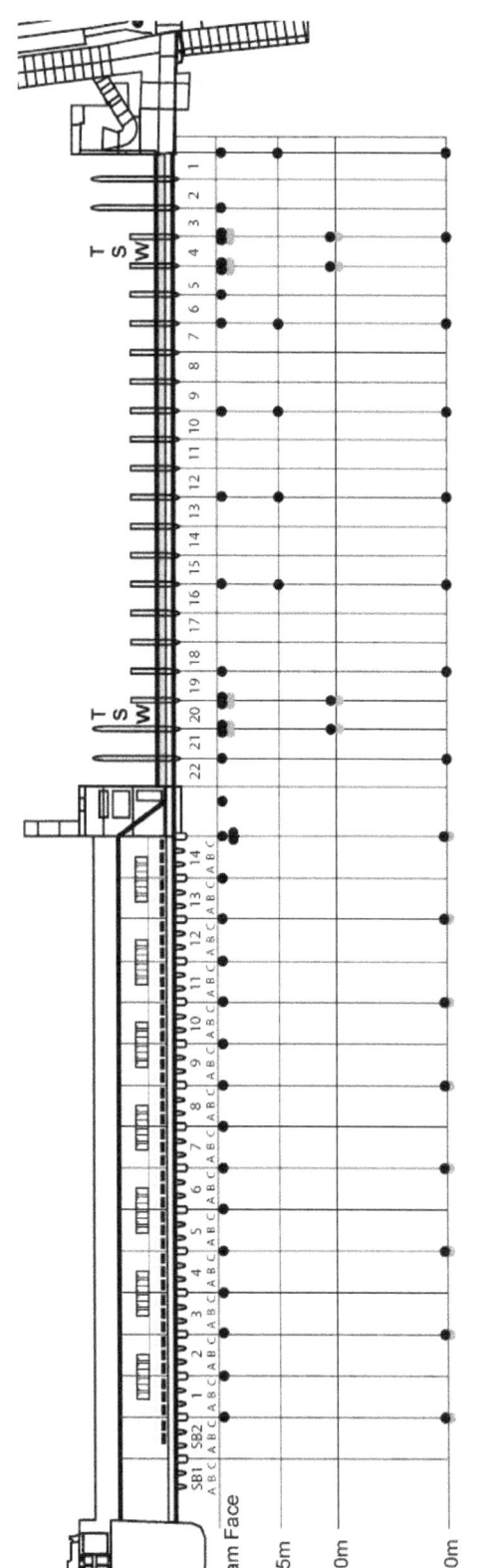
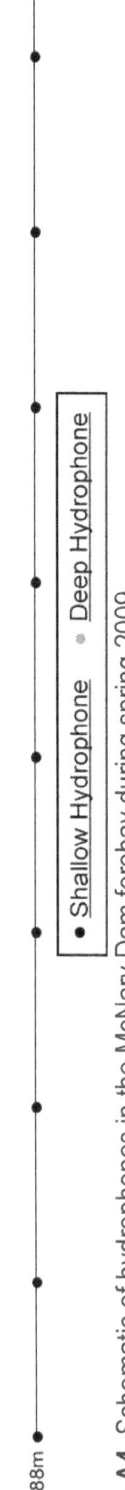

Figure A4. Schematic of hydrophones in the McNary Dam forebay during spring 2009.

• Shallow Hydrophone   • Deep Hydrophone

72

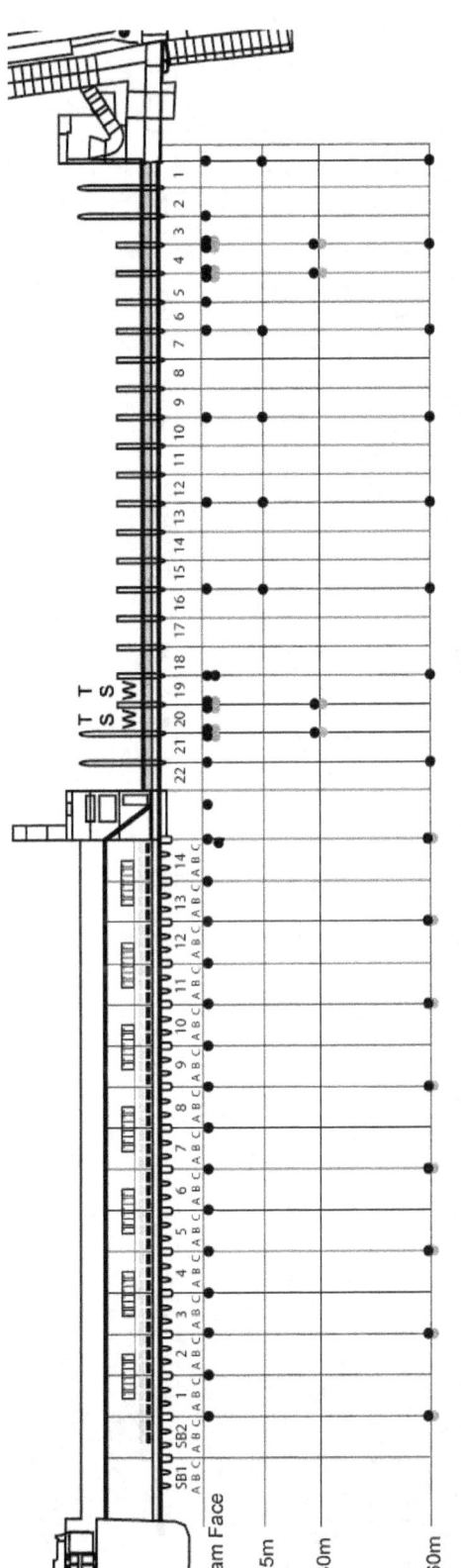
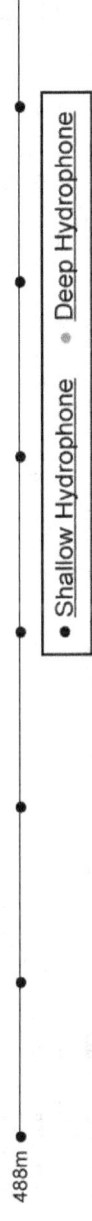

Figure A5. Schematic of hydrophones in the McNary Dam forebay during summer 2009.

● Shallow Hydrophone   ● Deep Hydrophone

Appendix B: Results from the 2006 to 2009 one-step Markov chain analysis for all fish regardless of where they first approached the dam during the day and night periods.

Table B1. Percentage of fish passing McNary Dam during day period in 2006 based on a one-step Markov Chain analysis.

[Data represent all fish regardless of where they first approached the dam during the day period. Species: YCH, Yearling Chinook salmon; STH, juvenile steelhead; SCH, subyearling Chinook salmon. Area of Passage: PH#1, turbine units 1–5; PH#2, turbine units 6–10; PH#3, turbine units 11–14; SP#1, spill bays 16–22; SP#2, spill bays 7–15; SP#3, spill bays 1–6; JBS, juvenile bypass system; Turb, turbine units; TSW, Temporary spillway weir; Bays, area spill bays. The (\) denotes the TSW was not installed at this time. Superscripts denote number of transitions used to calculate percentage, a > 100; b = 50 to 100; c = 10 to 50; (*) = < 10, which was insufficient sample size to calculate percentage]

								Area of Passage					
	PH #1		PH #2		PH #3		SP #1			SP #2	SP #3		
Species	JBS	Turbine	JBS	Turbine	JBS	Turbine	TSW 22	TSW 20	Bays	Bays	Bays	TSW 4	
YCH	13[a]	1[a]	15[a]	5[a]	15[a]	9[a]	\	\	79[a]	42[a]	57[b]	\	
STH	7[a]	4[a]	6[a]	2[a]	4[a]	3[a]	\	\	42[a]	24[a]	60[b]	\	
SCH	14[a]	10[a]	9[a]	11[a]	7[a]	12[a]	\	\	43[a]	40[b]	80[c]	\	

Table B2. Percentage of fish passing McNary Dam during night period in 2006 based on a one-step Markov Chain analysis.

[Data represent all fish regardless of where they first approached the dam during the night period. Species: YCH, Yearling Chinook salmon; STH, juvenile steelhead; SCH, subyearling Chinook salmon. Area of Passage: PH#1, turbine units 1–5; PH#2, turbine units 6–10; PH#3, turbine units 11–14; SP#1, spill bays 16–22; SP#2, spill bays 7–15; SP#3, spill bays 1–6; JBS, juvenile bypass system; Turb, turbine units; TSW, Temporary spillway weir; Bays, area spill bays. The (\) denotes the TSW was not installed at this time. Superscripts denote number of transitions used to calculate percentage, a > 100; b = 50 to 100; c = 10 to 50; (*) = < 10, which was insufficient sample size to calculate percentage]

								Area of Passage					
	PH #1		PH #2		PH #3		SP #1			SP #2	SP #3		
Species	JBS	Turbine	JBS	Turbine	JBS	Turbine	TSW 22	TSW 20	Bays	Bays	Bays	TSW 4	
YCH	24[a]	9[a]	20[a]	10[a]	21[a]	15[a]	\	\	82[b]	58[a]	61[b]	\	
STH	12[a]	3[a]	4[a]	1[a]	5[a]	2[a]	\	\	25[a]	19[a]	41[a]	\	
SCH	6[a]	10[a]	4[a]	9[a]	3[a]	4[a]	\	\	31[a]	31[b]	82[c]	\	

Table B3. Percentage of fish passing McNary Dam during day period in 2007 based on a one-step Markov Chain analysis.

[Data represent all fish regardless of where they first approached the dam during the day period. Species: YCH, Yearling Chinook salmon; STH, juvenile steelhead; SCH, subyearling Chinook salmon. Area of Passage: PH#1, turbine units 1–5; PH#2, turbine units 6–10; PH#3, turbine units 11–14; SP#1, spill bays 16–22; SP#2, spill bays 7–15; SP#3, spill bays 1–6; JBS, juvenile bypass system; Turb, turbine units; TSW, Temporary spillway weir; Bays, area spill bays. The (\) denotes the TSW was not installed at this time. Superscripts denote number of transitions used to calculate percentage, a > 100; b = 50 to 100; c = 10 to 50; (*) = < 10, which was insufficient sample size to calculate percentage]

		Area of Passage									
Species	PH #1		PH #2		PH #3		SP #1			SP #2	SP #3	
	JBS	Turbine	JBS	Turbine	JBS	Turbine	TSW 22	TSW 20	Bays	Bays	Bays	TSW 4
YCH	16[a]	4[a]	25[a]	3[a]	10[a]	9[a]	41[a]	17[a]	26[a]	39[a]	25[c]	\
STH	2[a]	1[a]	2[a]	0[a]	1[a]	1[a]	50[a]	17[a]	8[a]	4[a]	2[b]	\
SCH	24[a]	4[a]	23[a]	4[a]	5[a]	12[a]	44[a]	18[a]	21[a]	22[c]	*	\

Table B4. Percentage of fish passing McNary Dam during night period in 2007 based on a one-step Markov Chain analysis.

[Data represent all fish regardless of where they first approached the dam during the night period. Species: YCH, Yearling Chinook salmon; STH, juvenile steelhead; SCH, subyearling Chinook salmon. Area of Passage: PH#1, turbine units 1–5; PH#2, turbine units 6–10; PH#3, turbine units 11–14; SP#1, spill bays 16–22; SP#2, spill bays 7–15; SP#3, spill bays 1–6; JBS, juvenile bypass system; Turb, turbine units; TSW, Temporary spillway weir; Bays, area spill bays. The (\) denotes the TSW was not installed at this time. Superscripts denote number of transitions used to calculate percentage, a > 100; b = 50 to 100; c = 10 to 50; (*) = < 10, which was insufficient sample size to calculate percentage]

		Area of Passage									
Species	PH #1		PH #2		PH #3		SP #1			SP #2	SP #3	
	JBS	Turbine	JBS	Turbine	JBS	Turbine	TSW 22	TSW 20	Bays	Bays	Bays	TSW 4
YCH	22[a]	3[a]	22[a]	3[a]	12[a]	6[a]	43[a]	12[a]	27[a]	21[b]	29[c]	\
STH	7[a]	2[a]	7[a]	0[a]	6[a]	0[a]	33[a]	13[a]	10[a]	8[a]	32[c]	\
SCH	9[a]	6[a]	9[a]	5[a]	5[a]	5[a]	38[a]	20[a]	15[a]	16[b]	37[c]	\

75

Table B5. Percentage of fish passing McNary Dam during day period in 2008 based on a one-step Markov Chain analysis.

[Data represent all fish regardless of where they first approached the dam during the day period. Species: YCH, Yearling Chinook salmon; STH, juvenile steelhead; SCH, subyearling Chinook salmon. Area of Passage: PH#1, turbine units 1–5; PH#2, turbine units 6–10; PH#3, turbine units 11–14; SP#1, spill bays 16–22; SP#2, spill bays 7–15; SP#3, spill bays 1–6; JBS, juvenile bypass system; Turb, turbine units; TSW, Temporary spillway weir; Bays, area spill bays. The (|) denotes the TSW was not installed at this time. Superscripts denote number of transitions used to calculate percentage, a > 100; b = 50 to 100; c = 10 to 50; (*) = < 10, which was insufficient sample size to calculate percentage]

| | Area of Passage | | | | | | | | | | | |
| | PH #1 | | PH #2 | | PH #3 | | SP #1 | | | SP #2 | SP #3 | |
Species	JBS	Turbine	JBS	Turbine	JBS	Turbine	TSW 20	TSW 19	Bays	Bays	Bays	TSW 4
YCH	10[a]	5[a]	15[a]	7[a]	10[a]	13[a]	22[a]	24[a]	28[a]	7[b]	19[c]	\
STH	6[a]	1[a]	2[a]	1[a]	2[a]	5[a]	34[a]	20[a]	14[a]	4[b]	7[c]	\
SCH	10[a]	11[a]	5[a]	12[a]	2[a]	15[a]	18[a]	15[a]	40[a]	21[c]	46[c]	\

Table B6. Percentage of fish passing McNary Dam during night period in 2008 based on a one-step Markov Chain analysis

[Data represent all fish regardless of where they first approached the dam during the night period. Species: YCH, Yearling Chinook salmon; STH, juvenile steelhead; SCH, subyearling Chinook salmon. Area of Passage: PH#1, turbine units 1–5; PH#2, turbine units 6–10; PH#3, turbine units 11–14; SP#1, spill bays 16–22; SP#2, spill bays 7–15; SP#3, spill bays 1–6; JBS, juvenile bypass system; Turb, turbine units; TSW, Temporary spillway weir; Bays, area spill bays. The (|) denotes the TSW was not installed at this time. Superscripts denote number of transitions used to calculate percentage, a > 100; b = 50 to 100; c = 10 to 50; (*) = < 10, which was insufficient sample size to calculate percentage]

| | Area of Passage | | | | | | | | | | | |
| | PH #1 | | PH #2 | | PH #3 | | SP #1 | | | SP #2 | SP #3 | |
Species	JBS	Turbine	JBS	Turbine	JBS	Turbine	TSW 20	TSW 19	Bays	Bays	Bays	TSW 4
YCH	22[b]	5[b]	11[a]	7[a]	10[a]	14[a]	21[b]	21[b]	17[b]	12[c]	25[c]	\
STH	13[a]	4[a]	8[a]	2[a]	5[a]	7[a]	21[a]	11[a]	16[a]	12[b]	24[c]	\
SCH	13[a]	10[a]	6[a]	5[a]	3[a]	13[a]	20[b]	22[b]	22[b]	11[c]	20[c]	\

76

Table B7. Percentage of fish passing McNary Dam during day period in 2009 based on a one-step Markov Chain analysis.

[Data represent all fish regardless of where they first approached the dam during the day period. Species: YCH, Yearling Chinook salmon; STH, juvenile steelhead; SCH, subyearling Chinook salmon. Area of Passage: PH#1, turbine units 1–5; PH#2, turbine units 6–10; PH#3, turbine units 11–14; SP#1, spill bays 16–22; SP#2, spill bays 7–15; SP#3, spill bays 1–6; JBS, juvenile bypass system; Turb, turbine units; TSW, Temporary spillway weir; Bays, area spill bays. The (\) denotes the TSW was not installed at this time. Superscripts denote number of transitions used to calculate percentage, a > 100; b = 50 to 100; c = 10 to 50; (*) = < 10, which was insufficient sample size to calculate percentage]

	PH #1		PH #2		PH #3		SP #1			SP #2	SP #3	
Species	JBS	Turbine	JBS	Turbine	JBS	Turbine	TSW 20	TSW 19	Bays	Bays	Bays	TSW 4
YCH	17[a]	4[a]	12[a]	5[a]	20[a]	9[a]	21[a]	\	43[a]	53[a]	46[b]	27[b]
STH	7[a]	1[a]	6[a]	2[a]	5[a]	1[a]	39[a]	\	16[a]	13[a]	17[a]	31[a]
SCH	10[a]	7[a]	5[a]	6[a]	13[a]	14[a]	25[a]	18[a]	25[a]	51[a]	54[b]	0[b]

Table B8. Percent of fish passing McNary Dam during the night period in 2009 based on a one-step Markov Chain analysis.

[Data represent all fish regardless of where they first approached the dam during the night period. Species: YCH, Yearling Chinook salmon; STH, juvenile steelhead; SCH, subyearling Chinook salmon. Area of Passage: PH#1, turbine units 1–5; PH#2, turbine units 6–10; PH#3, turbine units 11–14; SP#1, spill bays 16–22; SP#2, spill bays 7–15; SP#3, spill bays 1–6; JBS, juvenile bypass system; Turb, turbine units; TSW, Temporary spillway weir; Bays, area spill bays. The (\) denotes the TSW was not installed at this time. Superscripts denote number of transitions used to calculate percentage, a > 100; b = 50 to 100; c = 10 to 50; (*) = < 10, which was insufficient sample size to calculate percentage]

	PH #1		PH #2		PH #3		SP #1			SP #2	SP #3	
Species	JBS	Turbine	JBS	Turbine	JBS	Turbine	TSW 20	TSW 19	Bays	Bays	Bays	TSW 4
YCH	12[a]	7[a]	13[a]	5[a]	19[a]	8[a]	22[a]	\	32[a]	51[a]	36[b]	29[b]
STH	10[a]	2[a]	7[a]	1[a]	9[a]	1[a]	20[a]	\	14[a]	26[a]	22[a]	27[a]
SCH	7[a]	8[a]	4[a]	8[a]	16[a]	17[a]	24[a]	24[a]	17[a]	44[a]	55[a]	0[a]

Appendix C: Results from the 2006 to 2009 two-step Markov chain analysis for all fish regardless of where they first approached the dam during the day and night periods.

Table C1. Percentage of fish passing McNary Dam during day period in 2006 based on a two-step Markov Chain analysis.

[Data represent all fish regardless of where they first approached the dam during the day period. Species: YCH, Yearling Chinook salmon; STH, juvenile steelhead; SCH, subyearling Chinook salmon. Area of Passage: PH#1, turbine units 1–5; PH#2, turbine units 6–10; PH#3, turbine units 11–14; SP#1, spill bays 16–22; SP#2, spill bays 7–15; SP#3, spill bays 1–6; Service Bay, equipment service bay on the south end of powerhouse; JBS, juvenile bypass system; Turb, turbine units; TSW, Temporary spillway weir; Bays, area spill bays. The (\) denotes the TSW was not installed at this time. Superscripts denote number of transitions used to calculate percentage, a > 100; b = 50 to 100; c = 10 to 50; (*) = < 10, which was insufficient sample size to calculate percentage]

Area of Passage:	PH #1						PH #2					
	passing PH#1 after coming from Service Bay		passing PH#1 after coming from forebay		passing PH#1 after coming from PH#2		passing PH#2 after coming from PH#1		passing PH#2 after coming from forebay		passing PH#2 after coming from PH#3	
Species	JBS	Turb	JBS	Turb	JBS	Turb	JBS	Turb	JBS	Turb	JBS	Turb
YCH	13[b]	3[b]	24[b]	0[b]	7[a]	1[a]	12[a]	5[a]	26[b]	8[b]	14[a]	3[a]
STH	0[c]	5[c]	19[c]	2[c]	2[b]	4[b]	6[a]	1[a]	16[c]	8[c]	3[a]	1[a]
SCH	15[a]	9[a]	23[a]	14[a]	9[a]	8[a]	7[a]	12[a]	16[a]	14[a]	8[a]	8[a]

Area of Passage:	PH #3						SP #1								
	passing PH#3 after coming from PH#2		passing PH#3 after coming from forebay		passing PH#3 after coming from SP#1		passing SP#1 after coming from PH#3			passing SP#1 after coming from forebay			passing SP#1 after coming from SP#2		
Species	JBS	Turb	JBS	Turb	JBS	Turb	TSW 22	TSW 20	Bays	TSW 22	TSW 20	Bays	TSW 22	TSW 20	Bays
YCH	13[a]	7[a]	20[b]	13[b]	0[c]	7[c]	\	\	86[a]	\	\	59[c]	\	\	76[c]
STH	2[a]	2[a]	13[c]	10[c]	2[c]	2[c]	\	\	48[a]	\	\	46[c]	\	\	21[c]
SCH	5[a]	9[a]	11[a]	19[a]	3[c]	7[c]	\	\	53[a]	\	\	18[c]	\	\	22[c]

Area of Passage:	SP #2			SP #3			
	passing SP#2 after coming from SP#1	passing SP#2 after coming from forebay	passing SP#2 after coming from SP#3	passing SP#3 after coming from SP#2		passing SP#3 after coming from forebay	
Species	Bays	Bays	Bays	Bays	TSW 4	Bays	TSW 4
YCH	39[c]	48[b]	31[c]	66[c]	\	50[c]	\
STH	24[b]	32[c]	10[c]	62[c]	\	*	\
SCH	49[b]	19[c]	*	91[c]	\	*	\

Table C2. Percentage of fish passing McNary Dam during night period in 2006 based on a two-step Markov Chain analysis.

[Data represent all fish regardless of where they first approached the dam during the night period. Species: YCH, Yearling Chinook salmon; STH, juvenile steelhead; SCH, subyearling Chinook salmon. Area of Passage: PH#1, turbine units 1–5; PH#2, turbine units 6–10; PH#3, turbine units 11–14; SP#1, spill bays 16–22; SP#2, spill bays 7–15; SP#3, spill bays 1–6; Service Bay, equipment service bay on the south end of powerhouse; JBS, juvenile bypass system; Turb, turbine units; TSW, Temporary spillway weir; Bays, area spill bays. The (\) denotes the TSW was not installed at this time. Superscripts denote number of transitions used to calculate percentage, a > 100; b = 50 to 100; c = 10 to 50; (*) = < 10, which was insufficient sample size to calculate percentage]

Area of Passage:	PH #1						PH #2					
	passing PH#1 after coming from Service Bay		passing PH#1 after coming from forebay		passing PH#1 after coming from PH#2		passing PH#2 after coming from PH#1		passing PH#2 after coming from forebay		passing PH#2 after coming from PH#3	
Species	JBS	Turb	JBS	Turb	JBS	Turb	JBS	Turb	JBS	Turb	JBS	Turb
YCH	24^b	10^b	42^b	16^b	11^a	5^a	11^a	6^a	42^b	20^b	12^b	5^b
STH	11^b	3^b	23^b	5^b	8^a	2^a	3^a	2^a	14^b	4^b	3^a	1^a
SCH	5^b	16^b	7^b	17^b	7^a	6^a	2^a	10^a	4^b	13^b	5^a	6^a

Area of Passage:	PH #3						SP #1								
	passing PH#3 after coming from PH#2		passing PH#3 after coming from forebay		passing PH#3 after coming from SP#1		passing SP#1 after coming from PH#3			passing SP#1 after coming from forebay			passing SP#1 after coming from SP#2		
Species	JBS	Turb	JBS	Turb	JBS	Turb	TSW 22	TSW 20	Bays	TSW 22	TSW 20	Bays	TSW 22	TSW 20	Bays
YCH	11^b	9^b	34^b	23^b	*	*	\	\	83^c	\	\	77^c	\	\	89^c
STH	3^a	1^a	9^b	11^b	9^a	0^a	\	\	27^a	\	\	29^c	\	\	21^a
SCH	3^a	4^a	3^b	7^b	0^c	0^c	\	\	39^b	\	\	0^c	\	\	23^c

Area of Passage:	SP #2			SP #3			
	passing SP#2 after coming from SP#1	passing SP#2 after coming from forebay	passing SP#2 after coming from SP#3	passing SP#3 after coming from SP#2		passing SP#3 after coming from forebay	
Species	Bays	Bays	Bays	Bays	TSW 4	Bays	TSW 4
YCH	75^c	60^b	42^c	64^c	\	59^c	\
STH	18^a	43^c	6^b	44^b	\	30^c	\
SCH	33^c	*	*	90^c	\	*	\

Table C3. Percentage of fish passing McNary Dam during day period in 2007 based on a two-step Markov Chain analysis.

[Data represent all fish regardless of where they first approached the dam during the day period. Species: YCH, Yearling Chinook salmon; STH, juvenile steelhead; SCH, subyearling Chinook salmon. Area of Passage: PH#1, turbine units 1–5; PH#2, turbine units 6–10; PH#3, turbine units 11–14; SP#1, spill bays 16–22; SP#2, spill bays 7–15; SP#3, spill bays 1–6; Service Bay, equipment service bay on the south end of powerhouse; JBS, juvenile bypass system; Turb, turbine units; TSW, Temporary spillway weir; Bays, area spill bays. The (\) denotes the TSW was not installed at this time. Superscripts denote number of transitions used to calculate percentage, a > 100; b = 50 to 100; c = 10 to 50; (*) = < 10, which was insufficient sample size to calculate percentage]

Area of Passage:	PH #1						PH #2					
	passing PH#1 after coming from Service Bay		passing PH#1 after coming from forebay		passing PH#1 after coming from PH#2		passing PH#2 after coming from PH#1		passing PH#2 after coming from forebay		passing PH#2 after coming from PH#3	
Species	JBS	Turb	JBS	Turb	JBS	Turb	JBS	Turb	JBS	Turb	JBS	Turb
YCH	15^b	6^b	23^a	6^a	14^a	3^a	22^a	2^a	36^a	3^a	22^a	4^a
STH	3^a	2^a	3^a	0^a	2^a	1^a	2^a	1^a	2^a	1^a	1^a	0^a
SCH	18^a	7^a	31^a	4^a	23^a	3^a	21^a	4^a	25^a	3^a	24^a	4^a

Area of Passage:	PH #3						SP #1								
	passing PH#3 after coming from PH#2		passing PH#3 after coming from forebay		passing PH#3 after coming from SP#1		passing SP#1 after coming from PH#3			passing SP#1 after coming from forebay			passing SP#1 after coming from SP#2		
Species	JBS	Turb	JBS	Turb	JBS	Turb	TSW 22	TSW 20	Bays	TSW 22	TSW 20	Bays	TSW 22	TSW 20	Bays
YCH	5^a	5^a	16^a	14^a	6^c	16^c	75^a	10^a	4^a	23^b	24^b	31^b	5^b	19^b	55^b
STH	1^a	1^a	2^a	0^a	0^b	1^b	74^a	8^a	2^a	18^b	27^b	9^b	15^a	32^a	23^a
SCH	4^a	11^a	6^a	11^a	0^c	17^c	62^a	10^a	15^a	23^b	25^b	32^b	0^c	42^c	16^c

Area of Passage:	SP #2			SP #3			
	passing SP#2 after coming from SP#1	passing SP#2 after coming from forebay	passing SP#2 after coming from SP#3	passing SP#3 after coming from SP#2		passing SP#3 after coming from forebay	
Species	Bays	Bays	Bays	Bays	TSW 4	Bays	TSW 4
YCH	39^c	39^a	42^c	31^c	\	23^c	\
STH	5^b	5^b	2^b	3^c	\	0^c	\
SCH	*	14^c	*	*	\	*	\

80

Table C4. Percentage of fish passing McNary Dam during night period in 2007 based on a two-step Markov Chain analysis.

[Data represent all fish regardless of where they first approached the dam during the night period. Species: YCH, Yearling Chinook salmon; STH, juvenile steelhead; SCH, subyearling Chinook salmon. Area of Passage: PH#1, turbine units 1–5; PH#2, turbine units 6–10; PH#3, turbine units 11–14; SP#1, spill bays 16–22; SP#2, spill bays 7–15; SP#3, spill bays 1–6; Service Bay, equipment service bay on the south end of powerhouse; JBS, juvenile bypass system; Turb, turbine units; TSW, Temporary spillway weir; Bays, area spill bays. The (\) denotes the TSW was not installed at this time. Superscripts denote number of transitions used to calculate percentage, a > 100; b = 50 to 100; c = 10 to 50; (*) = < 10, which was insufficient sample size to calculate percentage]

Area of Passage:	PH #1						PH #2					
	passing PH#1 after coming from Service Bay		passing PH#1 after coming from forebay		passing PH#1 after coming from PH#2		passing PH#2 after coming from PH#1		passing PH#2 after coming from forebay		passing PH#2 after coming from PH#3	
Species	JBS	Turb	JBS	Turb	JBS	Turb	JBS	Turb	JBS	Turb	JBS	Turb
YCH	24^c	7^c	35^b	4^b	13^a	1^a	20^a	1^a	24^b	4^b	24^a	5^a
STH	7^a	5^a	11^b	3^b	5^a	0^a	5^a	0^a	9^b	0^b	8^a	0^a
SCH	8^b	8^b	17^b	11^b	6^a	2^a	5^a	7^a	19^b	6^b	9^b	2^b

Area of Passage:	PH #3						SP #1								
	passing PH#3 after coming from PH#2		passing PH#3 after coming from forebay		passing PH#3 after coming from SP#1		passing SP#1 after coming from PH#3			passing SP#1 after coming from forebay			passing SP#1 after coming from SP#2		
Species	JBS	Turb	JBS	Turb	JBS	Turb	TSW 22	TSW 20	Bays	TSW 22	TSW 20	Bays	TSW 22	TSW 20	Bays
YCH	7^a	2^a	20^b	6^b	0^c	30^c	79^b	4^b	13^b	27^b	26^b	24^b	6^c	8^c	51^c
STH	5^a	0^a	16^b	0^b	5^b	0^b	49^a	13^a	4^a	19^c	12^c	7^c	10^b	13^b	23^b
SCH	5^a	4^a	3^b	7^b	8^c	12^c	49^a	15^a	13^a	34^b	23^b	18^b	9^c	28^c	16^c

Area of Passage:	SP #2			SP #3			
	passing SP#2 after coming from SP#1	passing SP#2 after coming from forebay	passing SP#2 after coming from SP#3	passing SP#3 after coming from SP#2		passing SP#3 after coming from forebay	
Species	Bays	Bays	Bays	Bays	TSW 4	Bays	TSW 4
YCH	36^c	20^c	12^c	*	\	18^c	\
STH	5^b	12^c	10^c	33^c	\	29^c	\
SCH	26^c	7^c	11^c	56^c	\	8^c	\

Table C5. Percentage of fish passing McNary Dam during day period in 2008 based on a two-step Markov Chain analysis.

[Data represent all fish regardless of where they first approached the dam during the day period. Species: YCH, Yearling Chinook salmon; STH, juvenile steelhead; SCH, subyearling Chinook salmon. Area of Passage: PH#1, turbine units 1–5; PH#2, turbine units 6–10; PH#3, turbine units 11–14; SP#1, spill bays 16–22; SP#2, spill bays 7–15; SP#3, spill bays 1–6; Service Bay, equipment service bay on the south end of powerhouse; JBS, juvenile bypass system; Turb, turbine units; TSW, Temporary spillway weir; Bays, area spill bays. The (\) denotes the TSW was not installed at this time. Superscripts denote number of transitions used to calculate percentage, a > 100; b = 50 to 100; c = 10 to 50; (*) = < 10, which was insufficient sample size to calculate percentage]

Area of Passage:	PH #1						PH #2					
	passing PH#1 after coming from Service Bay		passing PH#1 after coming from forebay		passing PH#1 after coming from PH#2		passing PH#2 after coming from PH#1		passing PH#2 after coming from forebay		passing PH#2 after coming from PH#3	
Species	JBS	Turb	JBS	Turb	JBS	Turb	JBS	Turb	JBS	Turb	JBS	Turb
YCH	14^c	3^c	9^c	4^c	10^b	6^b	13^a	8^a	29^c	2^c	7^b	9^b
STH	5^c	0^c	9^c	2^c	5^b	0^b	2^a	2^a	0^c	0^c	5^b	0^b
SCH	3^a	10^a	17^a	14^a	9^a	10^a	5^a	13^a	8^b	17^b	0^b	2^b

Area of Passage:	PH #3						SP #1								
	passing PH#3 after coming from PH#2		passing PH#3 after coming from forebay		passing PH#3 after coming from SP#1		passing SP#1 after coming from PH#3			passing SP#1 after coming from forebay			passing SP#1 after coming from SP#2		
Species	JBS	Turb	JBS	Turb	JBS	Turb	TSW 20	TSW 19	Bays	TSW 20	TSW 19	Bays	TSW 20	TSW 19	Bays
YCH	11^b	12^b	10^c	4^c	4^c	29^c	32^b	9^b	36^b	19^c	22^c	22^c	13^b	43^b	21^b
STH	3^a	3^a	1^b	2^b	3^b	11^b	45^a	17^a	14^a	16^c	16^c	8^c	5^b	34^b	20^b
SCH	3^a	12^a	0^c	12^c	0^c	27^c	20^a	13^a	44^a	24^c	16^c	29^c	4^c	21^c	43^c

Area of Passage:	SP #2			SP #3			
	passing SP#2 after coming from SP#1	passing SP#2 after coming from forebay	passing SP#2 after coming from SP#3	passing SP#3 after coming from SP#2		passing SP#3 after coming from forebay	
Species	Bays	Bays	Bays	Bays	TSW 4	Bays	TSW 4
YCH	0^c	8^c	10^c	*	\	16^c	\
STH	4^c	0^c	8^c	10^c	\	*	\
SCH	36^c	7^c	*	*	\	*	\

Table C6. Percentage of fish passing McNary Dam during night period in 2008 based on a two-step Markov Chain analysis.

[Data represent all fish regardless of where they first approached the dam during the night period. Species: YCH, Yearling Chinook salmon; STH, juvenile steelhead; SCH, subyearling Chinook salmon. Area of Passage: PH#1, turbine units 1–5; PH#2, turbine units 6–10; PH#3, turbine units 11–14; SP#1, spill bays 16–22; SP#2, spill bays 7–15; SP#3, spill bays 1–6; Service Bay, equipment service bay on the south end of powerhouse; JBS, juvenile bypass system; Turb, turbine units; TSW, Temporary spillway weir; Bays, area spill bays. The (\) denotes the TSW was not installed at this time. Superscripts denote number of transitions used to calculate percentage, a > 100; b = 50 to 100; c = 10 to 50; (*) = < 10, which was insufficient sample size to calculate percentage]

Area of Passage:	PH #1						PH #2					
	passing PH#1 after coming from Service Bay		passing PH#1 after coming from forebay		passing PH#1 after coming from PH#2		passing PH#2 after coming from PH#1		passing PH#2 after coming from forebay		passing PH#2 after coming from PH#3	
Species	JBS	Turb	JBS	Turb	JBS	Turb	JBS	Turb	JBS	Turb	JBS	Turb
YCH	10^c	10^c	30^c	7^c	20^c	2^c	8^b	8^b	8^c	8^c	18^c	6^c
STH	9^b	3^b	21^b	8^b	11^a	2^a	12^a	3^a	2^c	2^c	3^b	1^b
SCH	14^b	7^b	23^b	8^b	5^b	14^b	7^b	6^b	8^c	4^c	3^c	3^c

Area of Passage:	PH #3						SP #1								
	passing PH#3 after coming from PH#2		passing PH#3 after coming from forebay		passing PH#3 after coming from SP#1		passing SP#1 after coming from PH#3			passing SP#1 after coming from forebay			passing SP#1 after coming from SP#2		
Species	JBS	Turb	JBS	Turb	JBS	Turb	TSW 20	TSW 19	Bays	TSW 20	TSW 19	Bays	TSW 20	TSW 19	Bays
YCH	7^c	11^c	12^c	3^c	13^c	33^c	35^c	15^c	13^c	10^c	30^c	15^c	7^c	24^c	24^c
STH	4^a	4^a	11^b	0^b	4^b	19^b	25^a	8^a	19^a	3^c	13^c	13^c	16^b	18^b	11^b
SCH	4^b	9^b	4^c	9^c	0^c	29^c	24^b	18^b	26^b	24^c	14^c	5^c	8^c	35^c	27^c

Area of Passage:	SP #2			SP #3			
	passing SP#2 after coming from SP#1	passing SP#2 after coming from forebay	passing SP#2 after coming from SP#3	passing SP#3 after coming from SP#2		passing SP#3 after coming from forebay	
Species	Bays	Bays	Bays	Bays	TSW 4	Bays	TSW 4
YCH	14^c	6^c	17^c	*	\	*	\
STH	12^c	0^c	16^c	33^c	\	8^c	\
SCH	27^c	0^c	*	*	\	*	\

Table C7. Percentage of fish passing McNary Dam during day period 2009 based on a two-step Markov Chain analysis.

[Data represent all fish regardless of where they first approached the dam during the day period. Species: YCH, Yearling Chinook salmon; STH, juvenile steelhead; SCH, subyearling Chinook salmon. Area of Passage: PH#1, turbine units 1–5; PH#2, turbine units 6–10; PH#3, turbine units 11–14; SP#1, spill bays 16–22; SP#2, spill bays 7–15; SP#3, spill bays 1–6; Service Bay, equipment service bay on the south end of powerhouse; JBS, juvenile bypass system; Turb, turbine units; TSW, Temporary spillway weir; Bays, area spill bays. The (\) denotes the TSW was not installed at this time. Superscripts denote number of transitions used to calculate percentage, a > 100; b = 50 to 100; c = 10 to 50; (*) = < 10, which was insufficient sample size to calculate percentage]

Area of Passage:	PH #1						PH #2					
	passing PH#1 after coming from Service Bay		passing PH#1 after coming from forebay		passing PH#1 after coming from PH#2		passing PH#2 after coming from PH#1		passing PH#2 after coming from forebay		passing PH#2 after coming from PH#3	
Species	JBS	Turb	JBS	Turb	JBS	Turb	JBS	Turb	JBS	Turb	JBS	Turb
YCH	18^a	4^a	16^a	6^a	16^a	3^a	9^a	5^a	17^a	7^a	12^a	3^a
STH	7^b	1^b	4^b	0^b	8^a	1^a	6^a	2^a	9^b	5^b	5^a	1^a
SCH	10^a	6^a	20^b	8^b	5^a	7^a	3^a	5^a	10^a	7^a	3^a	8^a

Area of Passage:	PH #3						SP #1								
	passing PH#3 after coming from PH#2		passing PH#3 after coming from forebay		passing PH#3 after coming from SP#1		passing SP#1 after coming from PH#3			passing SP#1 after coming from forebay			passing SP#1 after coming from SP#2		
Species	JBS	Turb	JBS	Turb	JBS	Turb	TSW 20	TSW 19	Bays	TSW 20	TSW 19	Bays	TSW 20	TSW 19	Bays
YCH	19^a	6^a	23^a	15^a	14^c	14^c	21^a	\	56^a	25^b	\	35^b	12^c	\	26^c
STH	4^a	1^a	6^b	1^b	10^b	2^b	47^a	\	19^a	30^c	\	13^c	28^a	\	13^a
SCH	11^a	11^a	19^a	22^a	14^c	8^c	33^a	5^a	35^a	23^a	25^a	24^a	7^b	47^b	0^b

Area of Passage:	SP #2			SP #3			
	passing SP#2 after coming from SP#1	passing SP#2 after coming from forebay	passing SP#2 after coming from SP#3	passing SP#3 after coming from SP#2		passing SP#3 after coming from forebay	
Species	Bays	Bays	Bays	Bays	TSW 4	Bays	TSW 4
YCH	71^c	52^b	17^c	54^c	31^c	40^c	25^c
STH	17^b	19^b	3^b	14^b	37^b	22^b	22^b
SCH	55^b	51^b	43^c	55^c	0^c	53^b	0^b

Table C8. Percentage of fish passing McNary Dam during night period in 2009 based on a two-step Markov Chain analysis.

[Data represent all fish regardless of where they first approached the dam during the night period. Species: YCH, Yearling Chinook salmon; STH, juvenile steelhead; SCH, subyearling Chinook salmon. Area of Passage: PH#1, turbine units 1–5; PH#2, turbine units 6–10; PH#3, turbine units 11–14; SP#1, spill bays 16–22; SP#2, spill bays 7–15; SP#3, spill bays 1–6; Service Bay, equipment service bay on the south end of powerhouse; JBS, juvenile bypass system; Turb, turbine units; TSW, Temporary spillway weir; Bays, area spill bays. The (\) denotes the TSW was not installed at this time. Superscripts denote number of transitions used to calculate percentage, a > 100; b = 50 to 100; c = 10 to 50; (*) = < 10, which was insufficient sample size to calculate percentage]

Area of Passage:	PH #1						PH #2					
	passing PH#1 after coming from Service Bay		passing PH#1 after coming from forebay		passing PH#1 after coming from PH#2		passing PH#2 after coming from PH#1		passing PH#2 after coming from forebay		passing PH#2 after coming from PH#3	
Species	JBS	Turb	JBS	Turb	JBS	Turb	JBS	Turb	JBS	Turb	JBS	Turb
YCH	12^b	12^b	24^b	10^b	7^a	3^a	8^a	5^a	33^b	6^b	12^a	3^a
STH	9^a	3^a	12^a	4^a	9^a	1^a	5^a	1^a	16^b	5^b	7^a	1^a
SCH	5^a	6^a	11^b	15^b	5^a	6^a	2^a	8^a	6^b	10^b	5^a	7^a

Area of Passage:	PH #3						SP #1								
	passing PH#3 after coming from PH#2		passing PH#3 after coming from forebay		passing PH#3 after coming from SP#1		passing SP#1 after coming from PH#3			passing SP#1 after coming from forebay			passing SP#1 after coming from SP#2		
Species	JBS	Turb	JBS	Turb	JBS	Turb	TSW 20	TSW 19	Bays	TSW 20	TSW 19	Bays	TSW 20	TSW 19	Bays
YCH	14^a	1^a	25^b	17^b	27^c	16^c	25^b	\	41^b	18^b	\	37^b	23^b	\	16^b
STH	7^a	1^a	21^b	1^b	9^a	2^a	21^a	\	13^a	22^b	\	19^b	16^a	\	15^a
SCH	11^a	11^a	21^a	27^a	30^c	19^c	32^a	12^a	26^a	25^b	29^b	13^b	8^b	40^b	3^b

Area of Passage:	SP #2			SP #3			
	passing SP#2 after coming from SP#1	passing SP#2 after coming from forebay	passing SP#2 after coming from SP#3	passing SP#3 after coming from SP#2		passing SP#3 after coming from forebay	
Species	Bays	Bays	Bays	Bays	TSW 4	Bays	TSW 4
YCH	56^b	52^b	36^c	50^c	27^c	29^c	29^c
STH	24^a	41^a	14^b	25^a	27^a	12^c	27^c
SCH	53^b	43^a	36^c	59^b	0^b	52^b	0^b

Appendix D: Results from the 2006 to 2009 two-step Markov chain analysis for all fish that first approached the powerhouse during the day and night periods.

Table D1. Percentage of fish passing McNary Dam during day period in 2006 based on a two-step Markov Chain analysis.

[Data represent all fish that first approached the powerhouse during the day period. Species: YCH, Yearling Chinook salmon; STH, juvenile steelhead; SCH, subyearling Chinook salmon. Area of Passage: PH#1, turbine units 1–5; PH#2, turbine units 6–10; PH#3, turbine units 11–14; SP#1, spill bays 16–22; SP#2, spill bays 7–15; SP#3, spill bays 1–6; Service Bay, equipment service bay on the south end of powerhouse; JBS, juvenile bypass system; Turb, turbine units; TSW, Temporary spillway weir; Bays, area spill bays; NA, not applicable. The (\) denotes the TSW was not installed at this time. Superscripts denote number of transitions used to calculate percentage, a > 100; b = 50 to 100; c = 10 to 50; (*) = < 10, which was insufficient sample size to calculate percentage]

Area of Passage:	PH #1						PH #2					
	passing PH#1 after coming from Service Bay		passing PH#1 after coming from forebay		passing PH#1 after coming from PH#2		passing PH#2 after coming from PH#1		passing PH#2 after coming from forebay		passing PH#2 after coming from PH#3	
Species	JBS	Turb	JBS	Turb	JBS	Turb	JBS	Turb	JBS	Turb	JBS	Turb
YCH	13^b	3^b	24^b	0^b	7^a	1^a	12^a	5^a	26^b	8^b	13^a	2^a
STH	0^c	5^c	19^c	2^c	2^b	2^b	7^a	1^a	16^c	8^c	3^a	0^a
SCH	16^a	9^a	23^a	14^a	10^a	8^a	8^a	12^a	16^a	14^a	10^a	9^a

Area of Passage:	PH #3						SP #1								
	passing PH#3 after coming from PH#2		passing PH#3 after coming from forebay		passing PH#3 after coming from SP#1		passing SP#1 after coming from PH#3			passing SP#1 after coming from forebay			passing SP#1 after coming from SP#2		
Species	JBS	Turb	JBS	Turb	JBS	Turb	TSW 22	TSW 20	Bays	TSW 22	TSW 20	Bays	TSW 22	TSW 20	Bays
YCH	13^a	7^a	20^b	13^b	*	*	\	\	88^b	NA	NA	NA	\	\	*
STH	2^a	2^a	13^c	10^c	5^c	0^c	\	\	49^b	NA	NA	NA	\	\	21^c
SCH	5^a	10^a	11^a	19^a	*	*	\	\	55^b	NA	NA	NA	\	\	*

Area of Passage:	SP #2			SP #3			
	passing SP#2 after coming from SP#1	passing SP#2 after coming from forebay	passing SP#2 after coming from SP#3	passing SP#3 after coming from SP#2		passing SP#3 after coming from forebay	
Species	Bays	Bays	Bays	Bays	TSW 4	Bays	TSW 4
YCH	*	NA	*	*	\	NA	NA
STH	23^c	NA	*	57^c	\	NA	NA
SCH	57^c	NA	*	93^c	\	NA	NA

Table D2. Percentage of fish passing McNary Dam during night period in 2006 based on a two-step Markov Chain analysis.

[Data represent all fish that first approached the powerhouse during the night period. Species: YCH, Yearling Chinook salmon; STH, juvenile steelhead; SCH, subyearling Chinook salmon. Area of Passage: PH#1, turbine units 1–5; PH#2, turbine units 6–10; PH#3, turbine units 11–14; SP#1, spill bays 16–22; SP#2, spill bays 7–15; SP#3, spill bays 1–6; Service Bay, equipment service bay on the south end of powerhouse; JBS, juvenile bypass system; Turb, turbine units; TSW, Temporary spillway weir; Bays, area spill bays; NA, not applicable. The (\) denotes the TSW was not installed at this time. Superscripts denote number of transitions used to calculate percentage, a > 100; b = 50 to 100; c = 10 to 50; (*) = < 10, which was insufficient sample size to calculate percentage]

Area of Passage:	PH #1						PH #2					
	passing PH#1 after coming from Service Bay		passing PH#1 after coming from forebay		passing PH#1 after coming from PH#2		passing PH#2 after coming from PH#1		passing PH#2 after coming from forebay		passing PH#2 after coming from PH#3	
Species	JBS	Turb	JBS	Turb	JBS	Turb	JBS	Turb	JBS	Turb	JBS	Turb
YCH	24^b	10^b	42^b	16^b	10^a	5^a	11^a	6^a	42^b	20^b	12^b	5^b
STH	13^b	3^b	23^b	5^b	6^a	1^a	3^a	2^a	14^b	4^b	3^a	1^a
SCH	4^b	15^b	7^b	17^b	7^a	6^a	2^a	10^a	4^b	13^b	6^a	7^a

Area of Passage:	PH #3						SP #1								
	passing PH#3 after coming from PH#2		passing PH#3 after coming from forebay		passing PH#3 after coming from SP#1		passing SP#1 after coming from PH#3			passing SP#1 after coming from forebay			passing SP#1 after coming from SP#2		
Species	JBS	Turb	JBS	Turb	JBS	Turb	TSW 22	TSW 20	Bays	TSW 22	TSW 20	Bays	TSW 22	TSW 20	Bays
YCH	11^b	9^b	34^b	23^b	*	*	\	\	85^c	NA	NA	NA	\	\	*
STH	3^a	1^a	9^b	11^b	6^b	0^b	\	\	27^a	NA	NA	NA	\	\	25^b
SCH	3^a	4^a	3^b	7^b	*	*	\	\	39^b	NA	NA	NA	\	\	*

Area of Passage:	SP #2			SP #3			
	passing SP#2 after coming from SP#1	passing SP#2 after coming from forebay	passing SP#2 after coming from SP#3	passing SP#3 after coming from SP#2		passing SP#3 after coming from forebay	
Species	Bays	Bays	Bays	Bays	TSW 4	Bays	TSW 4
YCH	*	NA	*	*	\	NA	NA
STH	18^a	NA	9^c	42^b	\	NA	NA
SCH	32^c	NA	*	95^c	\	NA	NA

Table D3. Percentage of fish passing McNary Dam during day period in 2007 based on a two-step Markov Chain analysis.

[Data represent all fish that first approached the powerhouse during the day period. Species: YCH, Yearling Chinook salmon; STH, juvenile steelhead; SCH, subyearling Chinook salmon. Area of Passage: PH#1, turbine units 1–5; PH#2, turbine units 6–10; PH#3, turbine units 11–14; SP#1, spill bays 16–22; SP#2, spill bays 7–15; SP#3, spill bays 1–6; Service Bay, equipment service bay on the south end of powerhouse; JBS, juvenile bypass system; Turb, turbine units; TSW, Temporary spillway weir; Bays, area spill bays; NA, not applicable. The (\) denotes the TSW was not installed at this time. Superscripts denote number of transitions used to calculate percentage, a > 100; b = 50 to 100; c = 10 to 50; (*) = < 10, which was insufficient sample size to calculate percentage]

Area of Passage:	PH #1						PH #2					
	passing PH#1 after coming from Service Bay		passing PH#1 after coming from forebay		passing PH#1 after coming from PH#2		passing PH#2 after coming from PH#1		passing PH#2 after coming from forebay		passing PH#2 after coming from PH#3	
Species	JBS	Turb	JBS	Turb	JBS	Turb	JBS	Turb	JBS	Turb	JBS	Turb
YCH	15^b	6^b	23^a	6^a	14^a	3^a	22^a	3^a	36^a	3^a	21^a	3^a
STH	2^a	1^a	3^a	0^a	2^a	2^a	2^a	1^a	2^a	1^a	1^a	0^a
SCH	18^a	7^a	31^a	4^a	21^a	3^a	21^a	5^a	25^a	3^a	25^b	4^b

Area of Passage:	PH #3						SP #1								
	passing PH#3 after coming from PH#2		passing PH#3 after coming from forebay		passing PH#3 after coming from SP#1		passing SP#1 after coming from PH#3			passing SP#1 after coming from forebay			passing SP#1 after coming from SP#2		
Species	JBS	Turb	JBS	Turb	JBS	Turb	TSW 22	TSW 20	Bays	TSW 22	TSW 20	Bays	TSW 22	TSW 20	Bays
YCH	4^a	5^a	17^a	15^a	*	*	78^a	8^a	4^a	NA	NA	NA	*	*	*
STH	0^a	1^a	2^a	0^a	0^c	0^c	76^a	8^a	2^a	NA	NA	NA	10^c	25^c	10^c
SCH	5^a	11^a	7^a	11^a	0^c	17^c	63^a	11^a	14^a	NA	NA	NA	*	*	*

Area of Passage:	SP #2			SP #3			
	passing SP#2 after coming from SP#1	passing SP#2 after coming from forebay	passing SP#2 after coming from SP#3	passing SP#3 after coming from SP#2		passing SP#3 after coming from forebay	
Species	Bays	Bays	Bays	Bays	TSW 4	Bays	TSW 4
YCH	30^c	NA	*	*	\	NA	NA
STH	0^c	NA	0^c	6^c	\	NA	NA
SCH	*	NA	*	*	\	NA	NA

Table D4. Percentage of fish passing McNary Dam during night period in 2007 based on a two-step Markov Chain analysis.

[Data represent all fish that first approached the powerhouse during the night period. Species: YCH, Yearling Chinook salmon; STH, juvenile steelhead; SCH, subyearling Chinook salmon. Area of Passage: PH#1, turbine units 1–5; PH#2, turbine units 6–10; PH#3, turbine units 11–14; SP#1, spill bays 16–22; SP#2, spill bays 7–15; SP#3, spill bays 1–6; Service Bay, equipment service bay on the south end of powerhouse; JBS, juvenile bypass system; Turb, turbine units; TSW, Temporary spillway weir; Bays, area spill bays; NA, not applicable. The (\) denotes the TSW was not installed at this time. Superscripts denote number of transitions used to calculate percentage, a > 100; b = 50 to 100; c = 10 to 50; (*) = < 10, which was insufficient sample size to calculate percentage]

Area of Passage:	PH #1						PH #2					
	passing PH#1 after coming from Service Bay		passing PH#1 after coming from forebay		passing PH#1 after coming from PH#2		passing PH#2 after coming from PH#1		passing PH#2 after coming from forebay		passing PH#2 after coming from PH#3	
Species	JBS	Turb	JBS	Turb	JBS	Turb	JBS	Turb	JBS	Turb	JBS	Turb
YCH	22^c	7^c	35^b	4^b	14^a	1^a	21^a	1^a	24^b	4^b	24^b	5^b
STH	8^a	5^a	11^b	3^b	5^a	0^a	4^a	0^a	9^b	0^b	8^a	0^a
SCH	7^b	8^b	17^b	11^b	6^a	2^a	5^a	6^a	19^b	6^b	10^b	2^b

Area of Passage:	PH #3						SP #1								
	passing PH#3 after coming from PH#2		passing PH#3 after coming from forebay		passing PH#3 after coming from SP#1		passing SP#1 after coming from PH#3			passing SP#1 after coming from forebay			passing SP#1 after coming from SP#2		
Species	JBS	Turb	JBS	Turb	JBS	Turb	TSW 22	TSW 20	Bays	TSW 22	TSW 20	Bays	TSW 22	TSW 20	Bays
YCH	8^a	2^a	20^b	6^b	*	*	78^b	5^b	13^b	NA	NA	NA	*	*	*
STH	5^a	0^a	17^b	0^b	7^c	0^c	47^a	13^a	3^a	NA	NA	NA	9^c	15^c	21^c
SCH	5^a	4^a	3^b	7^b	*	*	48^b	16^b	13^b	NA	NA	NA	*	*	*

Area of Passage:	SP #2			SP #3			
	passing SP#2 after coming from SP#1	passing SP#2 after coming from forebay	passing SP#2 after coming from SP#3	passing SP#3 after coming from SP#2		passing SP#3 after coming from forebay	
Species	Bays	Bays	Bays	Bays	TSW 4	Bays	TSW 4
YCH	*	NA	*	*	\	NA	NA
STH	2^c	NA	7^c	38^c	\	NA	NA
SCH	28^c	NA	*	*	\	NA	NA

89

Table D5. Percentage of fish passing McNary Dam during day period in 2008 based on a two-step Markov Chain analysis.

[Data represent all fish that first approached the powerhouse during the day period. Species: YCH, Yearling Chinook salmon; STH, juvenile steelhead; SCH, subyearling Chinook salmon. Area of Passage: PH#1, turbine units 1–5; PH#2, turbine units 6–10; PH#3, turbine units 11–14; SP#1, spill bays 16–22; SP#2, spill bays 7–15; SP#3, spill bays 1–6; Service Bay, equipment service bay on the south end of powerhouse; JBS, juvenile bypass system; Turb, turbine units; TSW, Temporary spillway weir; Bays, area spill bays; NA, not applicable. The (\) denotes the TSW was not installed at this time. Superscripts denote number of transitions used to calculate percentage, a > 100; b = 50 to 100; c = 10 to 50; (*) = < 10, which was insufficient sample size to calculate percentage]

Area of Passage:	PH #1						PH #2					
	passing PH#1 after coming from Service Bay		passing PH#1 after coming from forebay		passing PH#1 after coming from PH#2		passing PH#2 after coming from PH#1		passing PH#2 after coming from forebay		passing PH#2 after coming from PH#3	
Species	JBS	Turb	JBS	Turb	JBS	Turb	JBS	Turb	JBS	Turb	JBS	Turb
YCH	15^c	4^c	9^c	4^c	11^b	7^b	13^b	9^b	29^c	2^c	9^c	13^c
STH	3^c	0^c	9^c	2^c	7^b	0^b	2^a	2^a	0^c	0^c	8^c	0^c
SCH	4^a	11^a	17^a	14^a	10^a	11^a	6^a	14^a	8^b	17^b	0^c	3^c

Area of Passage:	PH #3						SP #1								
	passing PH#3 after coming from PH#2		passing PH#3 after coming from forebay		passing PH#3 after coming from SP#1		passing SP#1 after coming from PH#3			passing SP#1 after coming from forebay			passing SP#1 after coming from SP#2		
Species	JBS	Turb	JBS	Turb	JBS	Turb	TSW 20	TSW 19	Bays	TSW 20	TSW 19	Bays	TSW 20	TSW 19	Bays
YCH	11^b	14^b	11^c	4^c	*	*	36^b	9^b	40^b	NA	NA	NA	*	*	*
STH	3^a	4^a	1^b	2^b	7^c	19^c	47^a	17^a	14^a	NA	NA	NA	*	*	*
SCH	3^a	13^a	0^c	13^c	0^c	18^c	19^a	13^a	45^a	NA	NA	NA	*	*	*

Area of Passage:	SP #2			SP #3			
	passing SP#2 after coming from SP#1	passing SP#2 after coming from forebay	passing SP#2 after coming from SP#3	passing SP#3 after coming from SP#2		passing SP#3 after coming from forebay	
Species	Bays	Bays	Bays	Bays	TSW 4	Bays	TSW 4
YCH	*	NA	*	*	\	NA	NA
STH	*	NA	*	*	\	NA	NA
SCH	39^c	NA	*	*	\	NA	NA

90

Table D6. Percentage of fish passing McNary Dam during night period in 2008 based on a two-step Markov Chain analysis.

[Data represent all fish that first approached the powerhouse during the night period. Species: YCH, Yearling Chinook salmon; STH, juvenile steelhead; SCH, subyearling Chinook salmon. Area of Passage: PH#1, turbine units 1–5; PH#2, turbine units 6–10; PH#3, turbine units 11–14; SP#1, spill bays 16–22; SP#2, spill bays 7–15; SP#3, spill bays 1–6; Service Bay, equipment service bay on the south end of powerhouse; JBS, juvenile bypass system; Turb, turbine units; TSW, Temporary spillway weir; Bays, area spill bays; NA, not applicable. The (\) denotes the TSW was not installed at this time. Superscripts denote number of transitions used to calculate percentage, a > 100; b = 50 to 100; c = 10 to 50; (*) = < 10, which was insufficient sample size to calculate percentage]

Area of Passage:	PH #1						PH #2					
	passing PH#1 after coming from Service Bay		passing PH#1 after coming from forebay		passing PH#1 after coming from PH#2		passing PH#2 after coming from PH#1		passing PH#2 after coming from forebay		passing PH#2 after coming from PH#3	
Species	JBS	Turb	JBS	Turb	JBS	Turb	JBS	Turb	JBS	Turb	JBS	Turb
YCH	10^c	10^c	30^c	7^c	17^c	2^c	8^b	6^b	8^c	8^c	15^c	7^c
STH	7^b	4^b	21^b	8^b	11^a	2^a	14^a	3^a	2^c	2^c	5^b	0^b
SCH	15^b	8^b	23^b	8^b	5^b	15^b	8^b	5^b	8^c	4^c	4^c	4^c

Area of Passage:	PH #3						SP #1								
	passing PH#3 after coming from PH#2		passing PH#3 after coming from forebay		passing PH#3 after coming from SP#1		passing SP#1 after coming from PH#3			passing SP#1 after coming from forebay			passing SP#1 after coming from SP#2		
Species	JBS	Turb	JBS	Turb	JBS	Turb	TSW 20	TSW 19	Bays	TSW 20	TSW 19	Bays	TSW 20	TSW 19	Bays
YCH	7^c	9^c	12^c	3^c	10^c	30^c	34^c	14^c	14^c	NA	NA	NA	*	*	*
STH	3^a	4^a	12^b	0^b	2^c	21^c	27^a	7^a	19^a	NA	NA	NA	29^c	24^c	6^c
SCH	2^b	10^b	5^c	9^c	*	*	26^c	16^c	21^c	NA	NA	NA	*	*	*

Area of Passage:	SP #2			SP #3			
	passing SP#2 after coming from SP#1	passing SP#2 after coming from forebay	passing SP#2 after coming from SP#3	passing SP#3 after coming from SP#2		passing SP#3 after coming from forebay	
Species	Bays	Bays	Bays	Bays	TSW 4	Bays	TSW 4
YCH	*	NA	*	*	\	NA	NA
STH	14^c	NA	*	50^c	\	NA	NA
SCH	25^c	NA	*	*	\	NA	NA

Table D7. Percentage of fish passing McNary Dam during day period in 2009 based on a two-step Markov Chain analysis.

[Data represent all fish that first approached the powerhouse during the day period. Species: YCH, Yearling Chinook salmon; STH, juvenile steelhead; SCH, subyearling Chinook salmon. Area of Passage: PH#1, turbine units 1–5; PH#2, turbine units 6–10; PH#3, turbine units 11–14; SP#1, spill bays 16–22; SP#2, spill bays 7–15; SP#3, spill bays 1–6; Service Bay, equipment service bay on the south end of powerhouse; JBS, juvenile bypass system; Turb, turbine units; TSW, Temporary spillway weir; Bays, area spill bays; NA, not applicable. The (\) denotes the TSW was not installed at this time. Superscripts denote number of transitions used to calculate percentage, a > 100; b = 50 to 100; c = 10 to 50; (*) = < 10, which was insufficient sample size to calculate percentage]

Area of Passage:	PH #1						PH #2					
	passing PH#1 after coming from Service Bay		passing PH#1 after coming from forebay		passing PH#1 after coming from PH#2		passing PH#2 after coming from PH#1		passing PH#2 after coming from forebay		passing PH#2 after coming from PH#3	
Species	JBS	Turb	JBS	Turb	JBS	Turb	JBS	Turb	JBS	Turb	JBS	Turb
YCH	18^a	4^a	16^a	6^a	16^a	3^a	9^a	5^a	17^a	7^a	9^a	3^a
STH	8^b	1^b	4^b	0^b	8^a	0^a	6^a	2^a	9^b	5^b	4^a	1^a
SCH	10^a	6^a	20^b	8^b	5^a	8^a	3^a	5^a	10^a	7^a	3^a	8^a

Area of Passage:	PH #3						SP #1								
	passing PH#3 after coming from PH#2		passing PH#3 after coming from forebay		passing PH#3 after coming from SP#1		passing SP#1 after coming from PH#3			passing SP#1 after coming from forebay			passing SP#1 after coming from SP#2		
Species	JBS	Turb	JBS	Turb	JBS	Turb	TSW 20	TSW 19	Bays	TSW 20	TSW 19	Bays	TSW 20	TSW 19	Bays
YCH	18^a	6^a	23^a	15^a	*	*	19^a	\	57^a	NA	\	NA	*	\	*
STH	4^a	1^a	5^b	1^b	3^c	3^c	46^a	\	20^a	NA	\	NA	24^c	\	21^c
SCH	11^a	11^a	19^a	22^a	21^c	0^c	33^a	4^a	34^a	NA	NA	NA	0^c	20^c	0^c

Area of Passage:	SP #2			SP #3			
	passing SP#2 after coming from SP#1	passing SP#2 after coming from forebay	passing SP#2 after coming from SP#3	passing SP#3 after coming from SP#2		passing SP#3 after coming from forebay	
Species	Bays	Bays	Bays	Bays	TSW 4	Bays	TSW 4
YCH	53^c	NA	*	*	*	NA	NA
STH	8^b	NA	0^c	12^c	39^c	NA	NA
SCH	45^c	NA	*	57^c	0^c	NA	NA

Table D8. Percentage of fish passing McNary Dam during night period in 2009 based on a two-step Markov Chain analysis.

[Data represent all fish that first approached the powerhouse during the night period. Species: YCH, Yearling Chinook salmon; STH, juvenile steelhead; SCH, subyearling Chinook salmon. Area of Passage: PH#1, turbine units 1–5; PH#2, turbine units 6–10; PH#3, turbine units 11–14; SP#1, spill bays 16–22; SP#2, spill bays 7–15; SP#3, spill bays 1–6; Service Bay, equipment service bay on the south end of powerhouse; JBS, juvenile bypass system; Turb, turbine units; TSW, Temporary spillway weir; Bays, area spill bays; NA, not applicable. The (\) denotes the TSW was not installed at this time. Superscripts denote number of transitions used to calculate percentage, a > 100; b = 50 to 100; c = 10 to 50; (*) = < 10, which was insufficient sample size to calculate percentage]

Area of Passage:	PH #1						PH #2					
	passing PH#1 after coming from Service Bay		passing PH#1 after coming from forebay		passing PH#1 after coming from PH#2		passing PH#2 after coming from PH#1		passing PH#2 after coming from forebay		passing PH#2 after coming from PH#3	
Species	JBS	Turb	JBS	Turb	JBS	Turb	JBS	Turb	JBS	Turb	JBS	Turb
YCH	12^b	10^b	24^b	10^b	7^a	2^a	8^a	5^a	33^b	6^b	10^a	3^a
STH	9^a	2^a	12^a	4^a	10^a	1^a	5^a	1^a	16^b	5^b	7^a	1^a
SCH	6^a	7^a	11^b	15^b	6^a	6^a	2^a	7^a	6^b	10^b	5^a	7^a

Area of Passage:	PH #3						SP #1								
	passing PH#3 after coming from PH#2		passing PH#3 after coming from forebay		passing PH#3 after coming from SP#1		passing SP#1 after coming from PH#3			passing SP#1 after coming from forebay			passing SP#1 after coming from SP#2		
Species	JBS	Turb	JBS	Turb	JBS	Turb	TSW 20	TSW 19	Bays	TSW 20	TSW 19	Bays	TSW 20	TSW 19	Bays
YCH	14^a	1^a	25^b	17^b	*	*	26^b	\	39^b	NA	\	NA	*	\	*
STH	6^a	1^a	21^b	1^b	2^b	2^b	21^a	\	13^a	NA	\	NA	15^b	\	14^b
SCH	11^a	10^a	21^a	27^a	33^c	8^c	34^a	10^a	27^a	NA	NA	NA	*	*	*

Area of Passage:	SP #2			SP #3			
	passing SP#2 after coming from SP#1	passing SP#2 after coming from forebay	passing SP#2 after coming from SP#3	passing SP#3 after coming from SP#2		passing SP#3 after coming from forebay	
Species	Bays	Bays	Bays	Bays	TSW 4	Bays	TSW 4
YCH	42^c	NA	*	*	*	NA	NA
STH	19^a	NA	17^c	20^b	26^b	NA	NA
SCH	28^c	NA	*	65^c	0^c	NA	NA

93

Appendix E: Results from the 2006 to 2009 two-step Markov chain analysis for all fish that first approached the spillway during the day and night periods.

Table E1. Percentage of fish passing McNary Dam during day period in 2006 based on a two-step Markov Chain analysis.

[Data represent all fish that first approached the spillway during the day period. Species: YCH, Yearling Chinook salmon; STH, juvenile steelhead; SCH, subyearling Chinook salmon. Area of Passage: PH#1, turbine units 1–5; PH#2, turbine units 6–10; PH#3, turbine units 11–14; SP#1, spill bays 16–22; SP#2, spill bays 7–15; SP#3, spill bays 1–6; Service Bay, equipment service bay on the south end of powerhouse; JBS, juvenile bypass system; Turb, turbine units; TSW, Temporary spillway weir; Bays, area spill bays; NA, not applicable. The (\) denotes the TSW was not installed at this time. Superscripts denote number of transitions used to calculate percentage, a > 100; b = 50 to 100; c = 10 to 50; (*) = < 10, which was insufficient sample size to calculate percentage]

Area of Passage:	PH #1						PH #2					
	passing PH#1 after coming from Service Bay		passing PH#1 after coming from forebay		passing PH#1 after coming from PH#2		passing PH#2 after coming from PH#1		passing PH#2 after coming from forebay		passing PH#2 after coming from PH#3	
Species	JBS	Turb	JBS	Turb	JBS	Turb	JBS	Turb	JBS	Turb	JBS	Turb
YCH	*	*	NA	NA	*	*	*	*	NA	NA	29^c	7^c
STH	*	*	NA	NA	0^c	14^c	0^c	0^c	NA	NA	5^c	5^c
SCH	*	*	NA	NA	4^c	16^c	0^c	5^c	NA	NA	0^c	6^c

Area of Passage:	PH #3						SP #1								
	passing PH#3 after coming from PH#2		passing PH#3 after coming from forebay		passing PH#3 after coming from SP#1		passing SP#1 after coming from PH#3			passing SP#1 after coming from forebay			passing SP#1 after coming from SP#2		
Species	JBS	Turb	JBS	Turb	JBS	Turb	TSW 22	TSW 20	Bays	TSW 22	TSW 20	Bays	TSW 22	TSW 20	Bays
YCH	*	*	NA	NA	*	*	\	\	*	\	\	59^c	\	\	78^c
STH	0^c	0^c	NA	NA	0^c	5^c	\	\	43^c	\	\	46^c	\	\	21^c
SCH	4^c	0^c	NA	NA	0^c	4^c	\	\	40^c	\	\	18^c	\	\	24^c

Area of Passage:	SP #2			SP #3			
	passing SP#2 after coming from SP#1	passing SP#2 after coming from forebay	passing SP#2 after coming from SP#3	passing SP#3 after coming from SP#2		passing SP#3 after coming from forebay	
Species	Bays	Bays	Bays	Bays	TSW 4	Bays	TSW 4
YCH	57^c	48^b	32^c	65^c	\	50^c	\
STH	27^c	32^c	9^c	67^c	\	*	\
SCH	33^c	19^c	*	*	\	*	\

Table E2. Percentage of fish passing McNary Dam during night period in 2006 based on a two-step Markov Chain analysis.

[Data represent all fish that first approached the spillway during the night period. Species: YCH, Yearling Chinook salmon; STH, juvenile steelhead; SCH, subyearling Chinook salmon. Area of Passage: PH#1, turbine units 1–5; PH#2, turbine units 6–10; PH#3, turbine units 11–14; SP#1, spill bays 16–22; SP#2, spill bays 7–15; SP#3, spill bays 1–6; Service Bay, equipment service bay on the south end of powerhouse; JBS, juvenile bypass system; Turb, turbine units; TSW, Temporary spillway weir; Bays, area spill bays; NA, not applicable. The (\) denotes the TSW was not installed at this time. Superscripts denote number of transitions used to calculate percentage, a > 100; b = 50 to 100; c = 10 to 50; (*) = < 10, which was insufficient sample size to calculate percentage]

Area of Passage:	PH #1						PH #2					
	passing PH#1 after coming from Service Bay		passing PH#1 after coming from forebay		passing PH#1 after coming from PH#2		passing PH#2 after coming from PH#1		passing PH#2 after coming from forebay		passing PH#2 after coming from PH#3	
Species	JBS	Turb	JBS	Turb	JBS	Turb	JBS	Turb	JBS	Turb	JBS	Turb
YCH	*	*	NA	NA	*	*	*	*	NA	NA	*	*
STH	0^c	0^c	NA	NA	21^c	3^c	8^c	0^c	NA	NA	3^b	2^b
SCH	*	*	NA	NA	10^c	10^c	0^c	7^c	NA	NA	0^c	5^c

Area of Passage:	PH #3						SP #1								
	passing PH#3 after coming from PH#2		passing PH#3 after coming from forebay		passing PH#3 after coming from SP#1		passing SP#1 after coming from PH#3			passing SP#1 after coming from forebay			passing SP#1 after coming from SP#2		
Species	JBS	Turb	JBS	Turb	JBS	Turb	TSW 22	TSW 20	Bays	TSW 22	TSW 20	Bays	TSW 22	TSW 20	Bays
YCH	*	*	NA	NA	*	*	\	\	*	\	\	77^c	\	\	92^c
STH	4^b	0^b	NA	NA	14^c	0^c	\	\	26^c	\	\	29^c	\	\	16^b
SCH	0^c	0^c	NA	NA	0^c	0^c	\	\	*	\	\	0^c	\	\	*

Area of Passage:	SP #2			SP #3			
	passing SP#2 after coming from SP#1	passing SP#2 after coming from forebay	passing SP#2 after coming from SP#3	passing SP#3 after coming from SP#2		passing SP#3 after coming from forebay	
Species	Bays	Bays	Bays	Bays	TSW 4	Bays	TSW 4
YCH	*	60^b	42^c	62^c	\	59^c	\
STH	17^c	43^c	3^c	48^c	\	30^c	\
SCH	40^c	*	*	*	\	*	\

Table E3. Percentage of fish passing McNary Dam during day period in 2007 based on a two-step Markov Chain analysis.

[Data represent all fish that first approached the spillway during the day period. Species: YCH, Yearling Chinook salmon; STH, juvenile steelhead; SCH, subyearling Chinook salmon. Area of Passage: PH#1, turbine units 1–5; PH#2, turbine units 6–10; PH#3, turbine units 11–14; SP#1, spill bays 16–22; SP#2, spill bays 7–15; SP#3, spill bays 1–6; Service Bay, equipment service bay on the south end of powerhouse; JBS, juvenile bypass system; Turb, turbine units; TSW, Temporary spillway weir; Bays, area spill bays; NA, not applicable. The (\\) denotes the TSW was not installed at this time. Superscripts denote number of transitions used to calculate percentage, a > 100; b = 50 to 100; c = 10 to 50; (*) = < 10, which was insufficient sample size to calculate percentage]

Area of Passage:	PH #1						PH #2					
	passing PH#1 after coming from Service Bay		passing PH#1 after coming from forebay		passing PH#1 after coming from PH#2		passing PH#2 after coming from PH#1		passing PH#2 after coming from forebay		passing PH#2 after coming from PH#3	
Species	JBS	Turb	JBS	Turb	JBS	Turb	JBS	Turb	JBS	Turb	JBS	Turb
YCH	*	*	NA	NA	*	*	*	*	NA	NA	41^c	6^c
STH	12^c	12^c	NA	NA	3^c	0^c	0^c	0^c	NA	NA	2^b	0^b
SCH	*	*	NA	NA	*	*	*	*	NA	NA	21^c	0^c

Area of Passage:	PH #3						SP #1								
	passing PH#3 after coming from PH#2		passing PH#3 after coming from forebay		passing PH#3 after coming from SP#1		passing SP#1 after coming from PH#3			passing SP#1 after coming from forebay			passing SP#1 after coming from SP#2		
Species	JBS	Turb	NA	NA	JBS	Turb	TSW 22	TSW 20	Bays	TSW 22	TSW 20	Bays	TSW 22	TSW 20	Bays
YCH	*	*	NA	NA	7^c	14^c	67^c	8^c	8^c	23^b	24^b	31^b	6^b	19^b	53^b
STH	2^c	0^c	NA	NA	0^b	2^b	58^b	8^b	2^b	18^b	27^b	9^b	16^a	34^a	26^a
SCH	*	*	NA	NA	0^c	17^c	*	*	*	21^b	26^b	33^b	0^c	44^c	19^c

Area of Passage:	SP #2			SP #3			
	passing SP#2 after coming from SP#1	passing SP#2 after coming from forebay	passing SP#2 after coming from SP#3	passing SP#3 after coming from SP#2		passing SP#3 after coming from forebay	
Species	Bays	Bays	Bays	Bays	TSW 4	Bays	TSW 4
YCH	46^c	39^a	44^c	20^c	\\	23^c	\\
STH	11^c	5^b	2^c	0^c	\\	0^c	\\
SCH	*	14^c	*	*	\\	*	\\

96

Table E4. Percentage of fish passing McNary Dam during night period in 2007 based on a two-step Markov Chain analysis.

[Data represent all fish that first approached the spillway during the night period. Species: YCH, Yearling Chinook salmon; STH, juvenile steelhead; SCH, subyearling Chinook salmon. Area of Passage: PH#1, turbine units 1–5; PH#2, turbine units 6–10; PH#3, turbine units 11–14; SP#1, spill bays 16–22; SP#2, spill bays 7–15; SP#3, spill bays 1–6; Service Bay, equipment service bay on the south end of powerhouse; JBS, juvenile bypass system; Turb, turbine units; TSW, Temporary spillway weir; Bays, area spill bays; NA, not applicable. The (\) denotes the TSW was not installed at this time. Superscripts denote number of transitions used to calculate percentage, a > 100; b = 50 to 100; c = 10 to 50; (*) = < 10, which was insufficient sample size to calculate percentage]

Area of Passage:	PH #1						PH #2					
	passing PH#1 after coming from Service Bay		passing PH#1 after coming from forebay		passing PH#1 after coming from PH#2		passing PH#2 after coming from PH#1		passing PH#2 after coming from forebay		passing PH#2 after coming from PH#3	
Species	JBS	Turb	JBS	Turb	JBS	Turb	JBS	Turb	JBS	Turb	JBS	Turb
YCH	*	*	NA	NA	*	*	*	*	NA	NA	20^c	10^c
STH	0^c	6^c	NA	NA	5^b	0^b	8^b	0^b	NA	NA	9^b	0^b
SCH	*	*	NA	NA	6^c	0^c	0^c	7^c	NA	NA	*	*

Area of Passage:	PH #3						SP #1								
	passing PH#3 after coming from PH#2		passing PH#3 after coming from forebay		passing PH#3 after coming from SP#1		passing SP#1 after coming from PH#3			passing SP#1 after coming from forebay			passing SP#1 after coming from SP#2		
Species	JBS	Turb	JBS	Turb	JBS	Turb	TSW 22	TSW 20	Bays	TSW 22	TSW 20	Bays	TSW 22	TSW 20	Bays
YCH	*	*	NA	NA	0^c	32^c	*	*	*	27^b	26^b	24^b	6^c	9^c	51^c
STH	8^c	0^c	NA	NA	3^c	0^c	65^c	15^c	0^c	19^c	12^c	7^c	11^b	11^b	25^b
SCH	*	*	NA	NA	12^c	0^c	*	*	*	34^b	23^b	18^b	12^c	36^c	16^c

Area of Passage:	SP #2			SP #3			
	passing SP#2 after coming from SP#1	passing SP#2 after coming from forebay	passing SP#2 after coming from SP#3	passing SP#3 after coming from SP#2		passing SP#3 after coming from forebay	
Species	Bays	Bays	Bays	Bays	TSW 4	Bays	TSW 4
YCH	36^c	21^c	13^c	*	\	18^c	\
STH	11^c	12^c	13^c	*	\	29^c	\
SCH	*	7^c	13^c	*	\	8^c	\

Table E5. Percentage of fish passing McNary Dam during day period in 2008 based on a two-step Markov Chain analysis.

[Data represent all fish that first approached the spillway during the day period. Species: YCH, Yearling Chinook salmon; STH, juvenile steelhead; SCH, subyearling Chinook salmon. Area of Passage: PH#1, turbine units 1–5; PH#2, turbine units 6–10; PH#3, turbine units 11–14; SP#1, spill bays 16–22; SP#2, spill bays 7–15; SP#3, spill bays 1–6; Service Bay, equipment service bay on the south end of powerhouse; JBS, juvenile bypass system; Turb, turbine units; TSW, Temporary spillway weir; Bays, area spill bays; NA, not applicable. The (\) denotes the TSW was not installed at this time. Superscripts denote number of transitions used to calculate percentage, a > 100; b = 50 to 100; c = 10 to 50; (*) = < 10, which was insufficient sample size to calculate percentage]

Area of Passage:	PH #1						PH #2					
	passing PH#1 after coming from Service Bay		passing PH#1 after coming from forebay		passing PH#1 after coming from PH#2		passing PH#2 after coming from PH#1		passing PH#2 after coming from forebay		passing PH#2 after coming from PH#3	
Species	JBS	Turb	JBS	Turb	JBS	Turb	JBS	Turb	JBS	Turb	JBS	Turb
YCH	*	*	NA	NA	0^c	0^c	18^c	0^c	NA	NA	6^c	0^c
STH	*	*	NA	NA	0^c	0^c	0^c	0^c	NA	NA	0^c	0^c
SCH	0^c	8^c	NA	NA	0^c	0^c	0^c	0^c	NA	NA	0^c	0^c

Area of Passage:	PH #3						SP #1								
	passing PH#3 after coming from PH#2		passing PH#3 after coming from forebay		passing PH#3 after coming from SP#1		passing SP#1 after coming from PH#3			passing SP#1 after coming from forebay			passing SP#1 after coming from SP#2		
Species	JBS	Turb	JBS	Turb	JBS	Turb	TSW 20	TSW 19	Bays	TSW 20	TSW 19	Bays	TSW 20	TSW 19	Bays
YCH	17^c	8^c	NA	NA	0^c	32^c	10^c	0^c	20^c	19^c	22^c	22^c	14^c	41^c	20^c
STH	4^c	0^c	NA	NA	0^c	5^c	35^c	19^c	16^c	16^c	16^c	8^c	6^c	27^c	21^c
SCH	0^c	10^c	NA	NA	0^c	29^c	25^c	8^c	33^c	24^c	16^c	29^c	5^c	23^c	41^c

Area of Passage:	SP #2			SP #3			
	passing SP#2 after coming from SP#1	passing SP#2 after coming from forebay	passing SP#2 after coming from SP#3	passing SP#3 after coming from SP#2		passing SP#3 after coming from forebay	
Species	Bays	Bays	Bays	Bays	TSW 4	Bays	TSW 4
YCH	*	8^c	10^c	*	\	16^c	\
STH	0^c	0^c	9^c	6^c	\	*	\
SCH	*	7^c	*	*	\	*	\

Table E6. Percentage of fish passing McNary Dam during night period in 2008 based on a two-step Markov Chain analysis.

[Data represent all fish that first approached the spillway during the night period. Species: YCH, Yearling Chinook salmon; STH, juvenile steelhead; SCH, subyearling Chinook salmon. Area of Passage: PH#1, turbine units 1–5; PH#2, turbine units 6–10; PH#3, turbine units 11–14; SP#1, spill bays 16–22; SP#2, spill bays 7–15; SP#3, spill bays 1–6; Service Bay, equipment service bay on the south end of powerhouse; JBS, juvenile bypass system; Turb, turbine units; TSW, Temporary spillway weir; Bays, area spill bays; NA, not applicable. The (\) denotes the TSW was not installed at this time. Superscripts denote number of transitions used to calculate percentage, a > 100; b = 50 to 100; c = 10 to 50; (*) = < 10, which was insufficient sample size to calculate percentage]

Area of Passage:	PH #1						PH #2					
	passing PH#1 after coming from Service Bay		passing PH#1 after coming from forebay		passing PH#1 after coming from PH#2		passing PH#2 after coming from PH#1		passing PH#2 after coming from forebay		passing PH#2 after coming from PH#3	
Species	JBS	Turb	JBS	Turb	JBS	Turb	JBS	Turb	JBS	Turb	JBS	Turb
YCH	*	*	NA	NA	*	*	*	*	NA	NA	*	*
STH	*	*	NA	NA	13^c	0^c	0^c	0^c	NA	NA	0^c	4^c
SCH	*	*	NA	NA	*	*	*	*	NA	NA	*	*

Area of Passage:	PH #3						SP #1								
	passing PH#3 after coming from PH#2		passing PH#3 after coming from forebay		passing PH#3 after coming from SP#1		passing SP#1 after coming from PH#3			passing SP#1 after coming from forebay			passing SP#1 after coming from SP#2		
Species	JBS	Turb	JBS	Turb	JBS	Turb	TSW 20	TSW 19	Bays	TSW 20	TSW 19	Bays	TSW 20	TSW 19	Bays
YCH	*	*	NA	NA	14^c	36^c	*	*	*	10^c	30^c	15^c	8^c	25^c	21^c
STH	5^c	0^c	NA	NA	5^c	16^c	16^c	12^c	16^c	3^c	13^c	13^c	11^c	16^c	13^c
SCH	*	*	NA	NA	0^c	25^c	*	*	*	24^c	14^c	5^c	11^c	37^c	37^c

Area of Passage:	SP #2			SP #3			
	passing SP#2 after coming from SP#1	passing SP#2 after coming from forebay	passing SP#2 after coming from SP#3	passing SP#3 after coming from SP#2		passing SP#3 after coming from forebay	
Species	Bays	Bays	Bays	Bays	TSW 4	Bays	TSW 4
YCH	*	6^c	*	*	\	*	\
STH	10^c	0^c	22^c	*	\	8^c	\
SCH	*	0^c	*	*	\	*	\

Table E7. Percentage of fish passing McNary Dam during day period in 2009 based on a two-step Markov Chain analysis.

[Data represent all fish that first approached the spillway during the day period. Species: YCH, Yearling Chinook salmon; STH, juvenile steelhead; SCH, subyearling Chinook salmon. Area of Passage: PH#1, turbine units 1–5; PH#2, turbine units 6–10; PH#3, turbine units 11–14; SP#1, spill bays 16–22; SP#2, spill bays 7–15; SP#3, spill bays 1–6; Service Bay, equipment service bay on the south end of powerhouse; JBS, juvenile bypass system; Turb, turbine units; TSW, Temporary spillway weir; Bays, area spill bays. ; NA, not applicable The (\) denotes the TSW was not installed at this time. Superscripts denote number of transitions used to calculate percentage, a > 100; b = 50 to 100; c = 10 to 50; (*) = < 10, which was insufficient sample size to calculate percentage]

Area of Passage:	PH #1						PH #2					
	passing PH#1 after coming from Service Bay		passing PH#1 after coming from forebay		passing PH#1 after coming from PH#2		passing PH#2 after coming from PH#1		passing PH#2 after coming from forebay		passing PH#2 after coming from PH#3	
Species	JBS	Turb	JBS	Turb	JBS	Turb	JBS	Turb	JBS	Turb	JBS	Turb
YCH	*	*	NA	NA	15^c	8^c	0^c	10^c	NA	NA	21^c	7^c
STH	0^c	0^c	NA	NA	9^c	6^c	7^c	0^c	NA	NA	11^c	0^c
SCH	*	*	NA	NA	*	*	*	*	NA	NA	0^c	10^c

Area of Passage:	PH #3						SP #1								
	passing PH#3 after coming from PH#2		passing PH#3 after coming from forebay		passing PH#3 after coming from SP#1		passing SP#1 after coming from PH#3			passing SP#1 after coming from forebay			passing SP#1 after coming from SP#2		
Species	JBS	Turb	JBS	Turb	JBS	Turb	TSW 20	TSW 19	Bays	TSW 20	TSW 19	Bays	TSW 20	TSW 19	Bays
YCH	38^c	6^c	NA	NA	11^c	14^c	*	\	*	25^b	\	35^b	10^c	\	25^c
STH	6^c	0^c	NA	NA	15^c	2^c	54^c	\	12^c	30^c	\	13^c	29^b	\	11^b
SCH	0^c	11^c	NA	NA	9^c	14^c	23^c	8^c	54^c	23^a	25^a	24^a	8^b	52^b	0^b

Area of Passage:	SP #2			SP #3			
	passing SP#2 after coming from SP#1	passing SP#2 after coming from forebay	passing SP#2 after coming from SP#3	passing SP#3 after coming from SP#2		passing SP#3 after coming from forebay	
Species	Bays	Bays	Bays	Bays	TSW 4	Bays	TSW 4
YCH	84^c	52^b	17^c	60^c	20^c	40^c	25^c
STH	30^c	19^b	4^b	16^b	35^b	22^b	22^b
SCH	69^c	51^b	46^c	53^c	0^c	53^b	0^b

Table E8. Percentage of fish passing McNary Dam during night period in 2009 based on a two-step Markov Chain analysis.

[Data represent all fish that first approached the spillway during the night period. Species: YCH, Yearling Chinook salmon; STH, juvenile steelhead; SCH, subyearling Chinook salmon. Area of Passage: PH#1, turbine units 1–5; PH#2, turbine units 6–10; PH#3, turbine units 11–14; SP#1, spill bays 16–22; SP#2, spill bays 7–15; SP#3, spill bays 1–6; Service Bay, equipment service bay on the south end of powerhouse; JBS, juvenile bypass system; Turb, turbine units; TSW, Temporary spillway weir; Bays, area spill bays; NA, not applicable. The (\) denotes the TSW was not installed at this time. Superscripts denote number of transitions used to calculate percentage, a > 100; b = 50 to 100; c = 10 to 50; (*) = < 10, which was insufficient sample size to calculate percentage]

Area of Passage:	PH #1						PH #2					
	passing PH#1 after coming from Service Bay		passing PH#1 after coming from forebay		passing PH#1 after coming from PH#2		passing PH#2 after coming from PH#1		passing PH#2 after coming from forebay		passing PH#2 after coming from PH#3	
Species	JBS	Turb	JBS	Turb	JBS	Turb	JBS	Turb	JBS	Turb	JBS	Turb
YCH	*	*	NA	NA	*	*	*	*	NA	NA	*	*
STH	7^c	3^c	NA	NA	6^b	0^b	7^c	0^c	NA	NA	5^b	0^b
SCH	*	*	NA	NA	*	*	*	*	NA	NA	*	*

Area of Passage:	PH #3						SP #1								
	passing PH#3 after coming from PH#2		passing PH#3 after coming from forebay		passing PH#3 after coming from SP#1		passing SP#1 after coming from PH#3			passing SP#1 after coming from forebay			passing SP#1 after coming from SP#2		
Species	JBS	Turb	JBS	Turb	JBS	Turb	TSW 20	TSW 19	Bays	TSW 20	TSW 19	Bays	TSW 20	TSW 19	Bays
YCH	*	*	NA	NA	25^c	21^c	*	\	*	18^b	\	37^b	26^b	\	16^b
STH	17^b	0^b	NA	NA	14^b	1^b	21^c	\	11^c	22^b	\	19^b	17^b	\	17^b
SCH	*	*	NA	NA	28^c	24^c	*	*	*	25^b	29^b	13^b	7^b	38^b	3^b

Area of Passage:	SP #2			SP #3			
	passing SP#2 after coming from SP#1	passing SP#2 after coming from forebay	passing SP#2 after coming from SP#3	passing SP#3 after coming from SP#2		passing SP#3 after coming from forebay	
Species	Bays	Bays	Bays	Bays	TSW 4	Bays	TSW 4
YCH	65^c	52^b	38^c	50^c	25^c	29^c	29^c
STH	37^c	41^a	11^b	32^b	27^b	12^c	27^c
SCH	71^c	43^a	39^c	56^c	0^c	52^b	0^b